THE UNITED STATES
IN A CHAOTIC WORLD

TEXTBOOK EDITION

∵

THE YALE CHRONICLES
OF AMERICA SERIES
ALLAN NEVINS
EDITOR

THE UNITED STATES IN A CHAOTIC WORLD

A CHRONICLE OF
INTERNATIONAL AFFAIRS, 1918–1933
BY ALLAN NEVINS

TORONTO: GLASGOW, BROOK & CO.
NEW YORK: UNITED STATES PUBLISHERS
ASSOCIATION, INC.

CONTENTS

I.	GUIDING TRADITIONS OF FOREIGN POL-ICY	Page	1
II.	THE LOST PEACE	"	27
III.	DOLLARS AND CENTS IN FOREIGN POL-ICY	"	62
IV.	PLANS FOR EXORCISING WAR	"	95
V.	THE TURN FOR THE WORSE	"	135
VI.	JAPAN DEFIES THE WORLD	"	169
VII.	THE AMERICAN NEIGHBORS	"	200
VIII.	THE BREAKDOWN OF DISARMAMENT	"	222
	BIBLIOGRAPHICAL NOTE	"	239
	INDEX	"	245

THE UNITED STATES

IN A CHAOTIC WORLD

. .

CHAPTER I

GUIDING TRADITIONS OF FOREIGN POLICY

AMERICANS little realized in the summer of 1914 that a series of events lay just ahead which would carry the republic into the very center of world affairs; which within a generation, indeed, would make the United States the chief leader in constructive international activities. How much preparation for that great role did America possess? Most citizens would have said very little. In the years following the First World War men frequently quoted with approval the absurd remark of Ambassador George Harvey that "the national American foreign policy is to have no foreign policy." The fact is that the United States has always had a foreign policy, though not always a good one. Like other nations, it has acted in the main upon motives of self-interest; like other nations, it has sometimes followed a course that was generous, bold, and helpful, and sometimes one that was selfish, evasive, and injurious to other lands. But its foreign policy has shown as much of consistent principle as that of any other government. While our course has necessarily been shaped in great part by immediate expediency, it cannot be understood without some attention to enduring American traditions.

The reasons why tradition counts for a good deal are several. The United States by 1926 was one hundred and fifty years old, had enjoyed a far longer continuous life under one form of government than any other great nation except Britain, and had had time to develop a distinct national personality. Its people have always been highly conscious of its history, and of a historic destiny among the nations of the globe. The country, too, has been protected from the kind of shocks which bring about rapid fluctuations in foreign policy. Because of its size, power, and relatively safe position it has had little reason to watch foreign capitals nervously or to fear sudden crises. It has therefore ordinarily been easier to predict the course of America, under given circumstances, than that of other great powers. For another reason, the general stability and conservatism of the American Government have made for stability in foreign affairs.

Down to the First World War, most Americans liked to believe that they stood aloof from the quarrelsome family of Old World nations and hence took comparatively little interest in external affairs. To the extent that it really existed, this indifference to foreign relations was not creditable. Its main source lay in the natural preoccupation of Americans with the development of their own rich domain. Among its other roots were sheer ignorance of other peoples, especially in frontier communities: a certain Fourth-of-July sense of superiority over countries not wise enough to adopt republican institutions and not full of business bustle; and a feeling of apprehension with regard to European leaders and diplomats as men too sophisticated, astute, and unscrupulous to be trusted by Americans. Yet this indifference could easily be overstated. In every generation many Americans had felt a passionate interest in international politics. This was natural in a nation of newspaper readers, highly common-schooled; a nation drawn from diverse sources, and maintaining numerous contacts with the lands of origin; a nation placed between Europe and the Orient, looking both East and West. In Washington's day even the masses were intensely aroused by the conflict between Britain and France. In Madison's time they were sucked into the final vortex of the Napoleonic Wars. In Monroe's day they were powerfully stirred by the Latin-American and Greek struggles for independence. So the story might have been pursued down to 1914. The second officer of government, so far as practical power and prestige go, has nearly always been the Secretary of State.

Moreover, a great change took place with the First World War. Before that conflict Americans were able to forget foreign affairs for considerable intervals. Wilson's first inaugural in 1913 contained not a line on the subject, and his message to Congress the following December referred only briefly to it. Beginning with the war, however, Americans grew far more conscious of the outside world. They set up important agencies for systematic study, such as the Council on Foreign Relations in New York City and the Foreign Policy Association, with headquarters in New York and branches elsewhere. A survey in 1930 of organizations for the study of international relations showed that more than 1,200 claimed a very considerable membership. In addition, such agencies as the Federation of Women's Clubs, Rotary, professional organizations, and various church bodies began to give a much larger place to the study of foreign affairs, while universities and colleges offered more and more courses. Important new libraries, like the Hoover Library at Stanford (devoted primarily to World War materials), were established, while schools of foreign relations were organized at several points.

All this, with the increased space given in American newspapers and magazines to able foreign correspondents, and the growing attention of radio commentators to foreign news, had a salutary effect. More and more people realized that Woodrow Wilson had spoken truly when he said in 1916 that America, instead of being a land of "provincial thinkers," ought to have the "broadest vision of any nation."

The first great tradition of the United States in ordering its foreign relations has been its disposition to support democracy, in the sense of popular self-government, throughout the world. The republic was born with the sense of a national mission. That mission was to assist in the diffusion of free political institutions. Imbued with this feeling, Americans have always been ready to denounce despotism, dictatorships, and other forms of repression. The same sentiment that nerved the patriots of 1776 to resist George III inspired Daniel Webster to taunt the despotism of Austria, Wilson to draw the sword against the autocracy of the German Empire, and Franklin D. Roosevelt to denounce the totalitarian states. Administrations in Washington were always quick to recognize republics set up by popular revolt, as in South America, always glad to welcome rebels like Kossuth, and always ready to send a word of cheer to oppressed peoples.

Historically, the attitude behind this tradition has undergone certain changes. During the first generation of the republic many American leaders were somewhat defiantly conscious that it was an experiment. As the experiment succeeded, Americans came during the next half-century to regard the nation as a great beacon light, a shining exemplar of democratic institutions in a benighted world. Lincoln expressed this sentiment at Gettysburg, when he said that government of the people, by the people, and for the people was undergoing its supreme trial. Later, especially when Wilson assumed national leadership, a host of Americans took a more crusading attitude; not merely by their example, but by their armed might, they would see that the world was made safe for democracy. It may be predicted that the United States will always show a strong hostility toward autocratic movements and a warm sympathy with democratic tendencies; and that when necessary it will become, as in 1914–18 and 1939–45, an arsenal for the protection of democracy overseas.

Another fixed tradition of American policy has been the avoidance of all needless entanglements with foreign nations. It is incorrect to say that the United States has generally pursued an isolationist policy; it has frequently done the precise opposite. But the nation has followed the broad lines of Washington's oft-misquoted advice in his Farewell

Address. He pointed out that Europe had a set of primary interests alien to those of America and fell into frequent controversies the causes of which did not concern the United States. "Hence, therefore, it must be unwise in us to implicate ourselves by artificial ties in the ordinary vicissitudes of her politics." But he said nothing about entangling alliances, a phrase coined later by Jefferson; and, indeed, although he warned his countrymen against permanent alliances, he specifically declared that they might "safely trust to temporary alliances for extraordinary purposes." He also made it clear that his predominant motive in counseling a cautious policy was "to gain time to our country to settle and mature its yet recent institutions." In short, he was for a reasonable avoidance of political connections with other lands, especially during the infancy of the republic, but he was not a dogmatic isolationist.

And, with some aberrations, America has followed the general policy defined by Washington. In its earliest years the nation made an alliance with France; after 1940 it made a practical defensive alliance with Canada. It has participated in three world-wide wars, those of 1812, 1917, and 1941. It annexed the Philippine archipelago far across the Pacific and took a historic stand as defender of the Open Door in China. Its sailors under Preble and Decatur fought to suppress the Barbary pirates; its forces nearly a century later helped suppress the Boxer Rebellion in China. It sent a squadron to Japan which by negotiated treaty opened that country to Western civilization. Its representatives took a leading part in the first Hague Conference in 1899, and again in the second Hague Conference in 1907. It has never been an isolated nation. But at the same time, it has always tried to avoid alliances, needless entanglements, and conflicts in the Old World.

A third guiding principle of American foreign policy has been offered by the Monroe Doctrine, with which we may couple the idea of Pan-Americanism. The Doctrine, promulgated when in 1823 Latin America seemed in danger of attack from a reactionary European combination, laid down two firm rules. They were, first, that the two American continents were no longer to be considered subject to colonization by any European nation; and second, that any interference with the new Latin-American republics for the purpose of controlling or oppressing them would be regarded as an unfriendly act toward the United States. It is clear that the Doctrine possessed great latitude and could be used to stop a wide variety of undertakings by European powers. The ordinary American, in fact, long thought of the Doctrine in excessively broad and vague terms. Having never studied its text, he has looked upon it as a general "Hands

Off!" warning. He has been so convinced that it is one of the bulwarks of American safety that he would tolerate no meddling with it, in the spirit of the citizen who exclaimed, "I don't know precisely what the Doctrine is, but I would die in its defense!"

In its original form, and during the period when the Latin-American republics were slowly growing to vigor, the Monroe Doctrine was necessary and wise. It served the republics by helping to keep them free from the intrigues and forays of rival European powers; it benefited the United States by protecting its southern flank. But the Doctrine was unfortunately given an interpretation by some Presidents which stretched it to cover improper objects. Moreover, as Argentina, Brazil, Chile, and other states grew to mature strength, they resented the aspect of a protectorate which the Doctrine bore. The defense of the Hemisphere, they maintained, should not be the business of Uncle Sam, but of all the republics acting jointly.

One of the unhappy extensions of the Monroe Doctrine was furnished by President Cleveland when he laid down the rule that if a European power holding New World territory had a boundary dispute with a Latin-American republic which it would not or could not settle by friendly means, then the United States had a right to step in and determine the boundary. Another corollary was invented by Theodore Roosevelt, who declared that whenever the government of a Latin-American nation became so disorderly, dishonest, or oppressive that European powers might be provoked to interfere on behalf of their nationals, the United States (since it forbade European interference) ought itself to exercise an international police power. This Roosevelt corollary provided a cloak for very dubious interventions. Another extension came from the Senate in 1912, when it passed a resolution asserting that no non-American "corporation or association" could be permitted to acquire an American harbor so situated that non-American naval or military forces there might threaten the United States. This was aimed at Japanese interests supposedly eyeing Magdalena Bay in Mexico.

The central object of Pan-Americanism had no necessary connection with the Monroe Doctrine. It was a movement intended to bring the American republics into a closer association for the promotion of trade, cultural interests, peace, and security. After 1900, many leaders of the United States favored the inclusion of Canada in the Pan-American system. It must be admitted that, although the ideal of Pan-Americanism dates back to the time of Henry Clay, it long made but slow progress. One obstacle lay in the fact that Latin America had always possessed much stronger ties, cultural, moral, and economic, with Continental Europe than with the United States. Another difficulty was found in the deep suspicion with which the United States was regarded by her southern neighbors. The Mexican War, the filibustering expeditions in the fifties, and some later episodes seemed proof of a predatory habit. After Theodore Roosevelt "took Panama," Yankee imperialism was widely feared. A third obstacle to the Pan-American movement lay in a pronounced difference in governmental ideals. While the people of the United States detested dictatorships, some Latin-American countries found them well adapted to their particular stage of political progress. Finally, and more fundamentally, in mind, temperament, and taste, Latin Americans differed radically from English-speaking Americans.

The early Pan-American Conferences accomplished little. The first was opened in Washington (1889) by Secretary Blaine, who hoped for an American *Zollverein*, a customs union which would increase trade within the Hemisphere and curtail that with Europe. Blaine also advocated the drafting of a plan for arbitrating all disputes. Both proposals were voted down; mutual jealousies among the Latin nations and a common distrust of the United States made them impracticable. The second and third Pan-American conferences failed to advance the arbitration proposals; for while Argentina led a group of nations which believed in compulsory arbitration, the United States, Mexico, and Brazil would accept only voluntary arbitration. The fourth conference in 1910 dealt only with secondary questions. When the fifth conference was held in Santiago in 1923, most Latin-American nations belonged to the League of Nations, whereas the United States did not; strong feeling had been kindled in South America by the intervention of Washington in several Caribbean republics; and Mexico and the United States were at loggerheads on important issues. As a result, the meeting proved abortive. When Dr. Brum of Uruguay proposed the continentalization of the Monroe Doctrine, the American delegates flatly rejected the idea. No agreement was reached as to arbitration. In all, the conference contrasted very unfavorably with what Europe was then accomplishing at Locarno and Geneva. The way was soon to open, however, for spectacular progress toward Pan-American unity.

A fourth basic tradition of American foreign policy could long have been defined as insistence upon the nation's freedom to navigate the seas in peace or war. This principle was made the second of Wilson's Fourteen Points; it has been resolutely upheld at all times except in two great crises—when Jefferson persuaded Congress in 1807 to pass the Embargo, and when Congress in 1935–37 passed laws giving up certain maritime rights. Both steps were taken in a desperate effort to keep the United States out of a world-wide conflict—and both failed. Secretary Henry L. Stimson in May, 1941, described the neutrality legislation of 1935–37 as "a violation of our most sacred and important tradition in foreign policy, the freedom of the seas," while Secretary Knox called it a "terrible blunder." But apart from these two interludes, America has vigorously maintained the principle.

The reason is simple. The United States has always been a strong mercantile nation, possessing an immense merchant fleet down to the Civil War, and one of considerable size at nearly all times. It has repeatedly been the principal neutral in a war-torn world. Naturally, it has stood for the right to send its goods and ships to every part of the globe without intolerable restrictions and seizures by belligerent powers. The Declaration of Paris in 1856 embodied a set of peculiarly American principles for which the United States had contended ever since its birth. Disagreement on one point only —the abolition of privateering—prevented America from accepting the Declaration of Paris. The historic American doctrines were that "free ships make free goods," cargoes of non-contraband aboard a neutral vessel not being subject to seizure even when owned by a belligerent; that contraband lists are limited to articles actually used in warfare; and that a blockade must be effective in order to be binding and must be maintained with due respect to neutral lives. The London Naval Convention of 1909 similarly embodied rules and definitions which corresponded with American views. It was largely in vindication of the freedom of the seas that the United States fought the War of 1812, and that it entered the First World War.

Another facet of the same tradition has been America's insistence upon the Open Door and upon the abolition of discriminations in maritime facilities. While the Open Door in China was first proposed by the British Government, Secretary John Hay took up the idea, pressed it upon other powers, and made it a temporary success. In general terms, Americans meant by the Open Door their right to sell goods, maintain industries, and make investments abroad on an equal footing with other foreigners. The principle applied to every nation, not merely to China. Any discrimination by Argentina or Switzerland in favor of Germans over Americans, or Britons over Americans, tended to arouse immediate indignation in the United States. So far as China went, custodianship of the Open Door was handed over to a group of nations by the Nine-Power Treaty of 1922; and when they failed to keep China open, most Americans regarded the defeat of the policy as merely temporary.

When the United States became independent, it found its trade hampered by the mercantilist restrictions of many nations and set itself to clear away as much of this jungle growth as possible. The Netherlands, for example, until 1852 refused to admit American vessels into the Dutch colonies in the New World. Various nations imposed lower tonnage dues on home ships than foreign ships, placed lower tariffs upon goods carried in national ships, and set up discriminations of other types. Ever since 1783 the United States has combated the international practice of such discriminations. By reciprocal legislation or formal treaty, by 1860 it had brought about the cessation of nearly all of them in direct trade and a great part of them in indirect trade. The United States has thus made a signal contribution to the death of mercantilism and to freedom of world intercourse. It has naturally condemned totalitarian practice in this field.

In dealing with tariffs, the United States has also consistently opposed discriminations. The ordinary provision of commercial treaties has been, in substance, that "the two parties shall enjoy in the ports of each other, in regard to commerce and navigation, the privileges of the most-favored nation." Many treaties of the nineteenth century were upon a conditional most-favored-nation basis. That is, they provided for certain special tariff rates on both sides which, being based on special bargains, did not automatically extend to other nations. But if these other nations made similar concessions, they could gain the special rates; so that the treaties were not really discriminatory. The principal later definition of American policy, that offered by the Reciprocal Tariff Act of 1934, permitted the President to negotiate trade agreements with other nations, reducing existing duties up to one half, and it extended gratuitously to all nations (unless they discriminated against the United States) every advantage offered by any reciprocal trade bargain. Discrimination was thus completely ruled out.

All in all, the United States has stood for unfettered freedom of commercial intercourse throughout the world. Following the Civil War, it set up high tariffs—often egregiously and foolishly high; and it, of course, never denied the right of other nations to set up such tariffs. But it has insisted that tariffs ought to apply to all alike, without special privilege for any. Needless to say, it has been sternly hostile to barter arrangements, the essence of which is discrimination and privilege. When Wilson in the third of his Fourteen Points called for the removal of economic barriers among nations, he was simply enunciating an old American doctrine.

So far as it has been guided by these basic principles—predilection for democracy, avoidance of needless entanglements, the Monroe Doctrine, the removal of commercial barriers—the foreign policy of the United States has been a mixture of caution and old-fashioned liberalism. The desire to support democracy, shown so vigorously in Clay's championship of the new Latin-American republics, in Webster's letter to Baron Hülsemann denouncing Austrian tyranny, and in a hundred other occurrences down to Franklin D. Roosevelt's attempts to check Hitler and Mussolini, was a liberal desire. The spirit of Pan-Americanism was a liberal spirit. America's belief in the Open Door and in freedom of the seas was a liberal belief. The spirit of Washington's warning about avoiding "artificial ties" and the "ordinary vicissitudes" of the Old World was a cautious spirit. The primary motive for the Monroe Doctrine was a defensive or cautious motive.

There have been darker phases in American policy, and it would falsify the picture not to indicate them. The United States has often played a creditable and even gallant role in world affairs; but it has sometimes played an exceedingly selfish and even predatory part. Perhaps the most dubious of its acts have related to the Latin-American neighbors which it ostensibly desired to protect.

The policy of territorial expansion which was consistently and aggressively followed until 1860 involved some unhappy episodes. On the whole, expansion to the Pacific was so inevitable and healthful that the term Manifest Destiny could well be applied to it. No objection could be entered to the

Louisiana purchase, or to the peaceful settlement of
the Oregon boundary, which gave the United States
the Northwest up to the 49th parallel. The annexation of Texas, at least as far as the Nueces, was also
a defensible act. But the Mexican War proved to be
a predatory war, and the annexation of the whole
northern third of what had been Mexico could be
justified only on the Carlylean principles that
might and right are interchangeable terms, and
that tools (and lands) belong to those who can
use them. One motive behind the War of 1812 was
the desire to seize Canadian soil, and American
armies invaded Canada with intentions that were
distinctly greedy.

After the Civil War national policy changed. An
effort by President Grant to bring about the annexation of Santo Domingo was condemned by
public opinion and effectively resisted by the
Senate. To be sure, the United States in 1867 did
purchase Alaska from Russia. But Alaska was part
of the North American Continent, it was virtually
unpopulated, and it was a natural appendage of the
United States. An effort by Republican leaders to
extend a protectorate over Nicaragua in 1884–85
was sharply halted when Grover Cleveland became
President in the latter year. A similar effort in
1892–93 to annex Hawaii was again halted by
Cleveland's reaccession to office. During the entire
period from the Civil War to the Spanish War the

American people seemed to be convinced that they should annex no territory outside the continent, no territory occupied by people of alien blood, language, and traditions, and no territory that had to be taken by force. Most Americans thought the national domain complete.

Then expansionist tendencies revived at the close of the century. The partitioning of Africa by the European powers had aroused in many Americans a desire for empire. A. T. Mahan preached not only the importance of sea power, but the duty of carrying civilization overseas. "Comparative religion teaches that creeds which reject missionary enterprise are foredoomed to decay," he wrote. "May it not be so with nations? . . . How much poorer would the world have been, had England heeded the cautious hesitancy that now bids us reject every advance beyond our shores." These sentiments fell pleasingly upon the ears of rising politicians like Theodore Roosevelt and Henry Cabot Lodge. The rise of a sensational press, with William Randolph Hearst as its worst and Joseph Pulitzer as its best exemplar, strengthened the appetite for a strenuous foreign policy. Many Christians liked the idea of carrying religious light to heathen areas. A feeling grew up among manufacturers and exporters that trade would follow the flag into new areas of the globe. The McKinley Administration witnessed the annexation of Hawaii, Puerto Rico, and the Philippines, while Cuba was placed under temporary American control followed by a protectorate.

The motives of the American people in this sudden expansion overseas were mixed. In so far as the United States was actuated by a desire to help take up the white man's burden in backward areas and to teach Christianity to pagan peoples, the impulse was good. In so far as the nation was actuated by jingoism, a feeling that it ought to boss some subject peoples, and a wish to swagger before other world powers, its course was bad. But the experiment was to be judged by results, and the nation soon decided that imperialism had been a mistake. Assurances of eventual independence were given the Filipinos by Democrats and Republicans alike, notably in the Jones Act of 1916. The assurances had a solid basis in American feeling that the Filipinos would be troublesome wards, and in a realization that, as Theodore Roosevelt had stated, the islands were strategically an Achilles' heel. Our desire to release the islands was soon strengthened by the hostility of American farmers to the unimpeded entry of Philippine agricultural exports.

Meanwhile, the United States had been accused, and not without some basis, of improper economic and financial expansion. The term "dollar diplomacy" was generally associated with the Taft Administration (1909–13), and by the term was meant an effort to assist or encourage American capital to flow into areas it would not otherwise enter. It was in the Far East that "dollar diplomacy" was most actively pursued. Its main political objective there was to bolster up the political integrity of China—certainly a commendable aim. In Latin America, "dollar diplomacy" was most conspicuously applied to the Caribbean area, and particularly to Central America. There its main political objective was the safeguarding of the Panama lifeline of the United States. Secretary Knox declared in a speech to the New York Bar Association that the construction of the Canal made the safety, peace, and prosperity of Central America and the zone of the Caribbean of paramount interest to the American Government. It was precisely in this region, he said, that the malady of revolutions and financial collapse was most dangerous; and it was for American investors, supported by the State Department, to apply a remedy. Unquestionably, under Taft this policy of supporting American bankers and traders was pushed much too far. In Nicaragua, in especial, the United States carried matters with a high hand.

But the American policy in Nicaragua and a somewhat similar course in Haiti were substantially the only important instances of "dollar diplomacy" in the proper sense of the term in the Western Hemisphere. When Woodrow Wilson came into power, he announced that in foreign affairs the Administration would not support any "special group of interests." His antagonism to the Taft-Knox policy was warmly applauded by the liberal press, and he did his utmost to maintain a correct line of conduct. It is true that he was soon forced to intervene to restore order in various little republics about the Caribbean; indeed, he carried out more armed interventions than any previous President. But he did not intervene in behalf of bankers or industrialists. He sent troops into Haiti in 1915 only when a long series of revolutionary disturbances culminated in an especially gory massacre and the lynching of the President by a frenzied mob. Marines likewise went into Santo Domingo, while troops were temporarily ordered into Mexico. They were retained in Nicaragua. But not the slightest evidence exists that predatory economic interests profited, except indirectly and unavoidably, from Wilson's acts. He never ceased to show his suspicion of such interests, and his desire to deal fairly with Latin America.

On the whole, the guiding traditions of American foreign policy toward Latin America have been friendly and helpful, and in the end they were destined to bear valuable fruit. Equally happy has been the guiding tradition of the United States toward the British family of nations, especially since the close of the nineteenth century.

Historically, America's most important foreign

relations have been those with the British Commonwealth and Empire. The longest land boundary of the United States has been shared with Canada, and Canadian foreign policy was long controlled from London. British sea power has always been a primary factor in the American outlook abroad. Sometimes it has been disadvantageous to the United States, as in the Napoleonic Wars; sometimes advantageous, as during the long decades when it was the real bulwark of the Monroe Doctrine. American commercial relations with the Empire have always been far greater than with any other power. With the young Dominions the people of the United States have always felt a special kinship. British ill-will and British good-will, for the simple reason that American civilization has largely a British mold, has always meant much to Americans. From the time that John Adams was sent to the Court of St. James's as the republic's first Minister, the London post has been the most prized and conspicuous in the American diplomatic service.

The foundations for a cordial partnership between America and Britain were laid at the turn of the nineteenth century. For a brief period late in 1895 relations between the two governments could apparently not have been worse. Yet the Venezuela affair of that year ended not merely peaceably, but with an enhancement of friendliness on both sides; and this was but the beginning. In the next ten years a series of events brought about a striking Anglo-American rapprochement, with a basis that was practical, not sentimental. The United States, as it annexed distant islands and became a true world power, realized that it needed British support. Great Britain, simultaneously disturbed by the rise of Germany as a threatening rival, realized that it needed American amity.

Three main steps drew the two countries into cordial relations before the First World War and thus made possible their cooperation in 1917–18 in defeating Germany.

1. When the United States went to war with Spain in April, 1898, Great Britain displayed the warmest sympathy. While Continental Europe for the most part desired a Spanish victory, London at once bloomed with American flags, and the British Government discouraged intervention by Germany and other European nations.

2. Immediately after the Spanish War, the United States and Great Britain formulated the Open Door policy in China. The British Government first proposed it, and two Britons, Lord Charles Beresford and Arthur E. Hippisley, did much to convert Washington to its adoption. Throughout the world, America and Britain stood for the preservation of equal trade privileges for all. Britain's own low tariff policy made her increasingly a market for American manufactured goods,

as she had always been a market for American raw materials.

3. The British Government made a series of diplomatic concessions to the United States which contributed greatly to good-will. At the beginning of the century it consented to abrogation of the Clayton-Bulwer Treaty under which Britain and America were to have equal privileges in any Isthmian Canal, neither to fortify or to enjoy exclusive control over it. Shortly afterward, Great Britain took a course in the Venezuelan debt question which again pleased the United States. Later still the British Government assisted in a settlement of the Canadian-Alaskan boundary which highly gratified the American people. The question was whether the undetermined line ran around the heads of certain inlets on the Pacific Coast, as Americans asserted, or across the heads, as Canadians contended. The matter was referred to a panel of jurists representing Canada, the United States, and Great Britain; the British jurist, Lord Alverstone, consistently voted with the American representatives and against the Canadians—as justice demanded.

These events strongly reinforced the ties knit by blood, literature, law, and common traditions between the two branches of the English-speaking race. They were further strengthened by another consideration. American and British life were steadily becoming more similar. As the United States became a great industrial democracy, it faced many of the special problems of urban industrialization that the British had earlier met. In dealing with these problems it drew heavily on British experience. The measures of social welfare undertaken by Theodore Roosevelt, Woodrow Wilson, and Franklin D. Roosevelt owed much to British precedent. At the same time, Great Britain was becoming socially and politically far more of a democracy than it had been during the nineteenth century. It drew heavily on American principles and ideals of democracy. An understanding of this growing similarity in ways and institutions contributed to the harmony of the two peoples. By 1920 it could be said that Anglo-American amity, no less than Pan-American amity, was one of the guiding traditions of American foreign policy.

CHAPTER II

THE LOST PEACE

DURING four centuries, down to the conflict of 1914, the European world had lived under a special system. It was a system in which the sovereign state was supreme, international ideals were few and weak, and mutual fear, suspicion, and jealousy produced over long periods what the philosopher Hobbes had called an almost chronic condition of war. During the nineteenth century peaceful ideals seemed gaining ground; but the peace was uncertain, and was maintained only by a balance of power. The ruling genius of these four centuries often appeared to be Machiavelli, whose ideas had become influential at the same time as the sovereign state. The dominant theme was international confusion, sometimes degenerating into anarchy. Very naturally, the American people, sundered from this turbulent system by three thousand miles of sea, wished to maintain a safe distance. Though more than once when the European balance was threatened the United States was called in to help restore it, the republic in general held itself aloof. Its attitude was modified only after 1880, when irresistible forces slowly brought America into the full stream of world affairs.

Then, shocked by the fearful calamity of the First World War, the nations reacted with spasmodic energy against the system which had given them such a tragic history. The ancient ideal of a world order was reinstated. Primarily under the leadership of Woodrow Wilson, a brilliantly hopeful scheme of collective security, the League of Nations, was organized at Paris. From that moment two great questions were posed to the world. Could the powers so far overcome their old habits of antagonism and aggression as to submit to a genuine international regime? Could the United States so far overcome its inveterate suspicion of the European temper as to join with the Old World in maintaining and strengthening the League system? The two questions were obviously interrelated. If Europe showed a new spirit of order and cooperation, the United States would be more likely to support the League and its work; if the United States consented to buttress the League, Europe would be more likely to manifest a changed temper.

As originally formed, the League was to include a number of neutral countries and all the nations which had declared war against Germany, while it was open to any fully self-governing state, domin-

ion, or colony which would furnish effective guarantees of an intention to observe its international
obligations and to obey the League's regulations as
to armaments. Three primary League organs were
created. One was the Assembly, in which each
member-state had one vote and which could deal
with any matter affecting the peace of the world.
One was the Council, which was to consist of the
United States, Great Britain, Japan, France, and
Italy as permanent members, with four non-per-
manent members to be elected at intervals by the
Assembly. The Council was to meet at least once
annually; the Assembly "from time to time." The
third organ was the Secretariat of the League, a
continuing and, as it proved, an important body.

The principal purposes and objects of the League
were embodied in a series of carefully written articles. The most important, Article Ten, required signatories to respect and preserve against external
aggression the territorial integrity and political
independence of all League members. Article Eleven
provided that, when any war or threat of war arose,
the Council should meet immediately and take
whatever action seemed best "to safeguard the
peace of nations." Succeeding articles stipulated
that members must submit any dispute likely to
cause war to adjudication, arbitration, or to a
Council inquiry, and must not commence hostilities
until at least three months after the arbitral tri-

bunal or Council had reported. Any member which should go to war without meeting its obligation for submission of the dispute to arbitration, judicial action, or the Council, would expose itself to severe economic sanctions in the severance of all trade, financial relations, and ordinary intercourse with member-states. Other articles authorized the Council to lay plans for the establishment of a Permanent Court of International Justice; created a system of mandates for former German- and Turkish-ruled territories; and outlined a broad program of social and humanitarian work.

Clearly, the League marked an epochal step forward in the effective organization of world peace, the restraint of aggressors, and the promotion of reform and humanitarian activity on an international scale. When it began its work (January 10, 1920), its roster included Great Britain and her Dominions, France, Italy, and sixteen other countries, including nine of Latin America. Yet it was far from being a powerful body. Most nations of Continental Europe had little faith in its ability to prevent war. Premier Clemenceau of France said frankly, "I like the League but I do not believe in it." Great Britain, which would have preferred a Covenant with fewer binding obligations than those upon which President Wilson insisted, regarded its activities with a mixture of hope and caution. Various smaller nations, like Argentina, were ready to support the League when it served their purposes, but to withdraw when it did not. And a heavy blow was delivered to the whole structure reared on the Covenant when the United States Senate, by a vote of 55 yeas to 39 nays late in 1919, and of 45 yeas to 39 nays early in 1920, failed to muster the two-thirds required for ratification. These votes were not regarded as final, for many indices of public opinion showed that a majority of Americans desired membership. The Presidential campaign of 1920 was at hand, and the League issue seemed certain to be carried into the thick of the party battle.

The reasons which lay behind the Senate's refusal to accept the League were numerous, complex, and in part deeply rooted in the nation's history. Isolationism from Europe was an old American tradition; President Wilson himself had been intent upon an almost exclusive domestic program when he entered office, while Secretary of State Bryan had been semi-isolationist as well as pacifist in his views. The four years during which advocacy of some form of league to enforce peace had been maintained, 1915–18, constituted too brief a period to permit of a deep and lasting impression on the national mind. President Wilson had become a champion of the idea in 1916, but his support was not impassioned until a year later. The conflict itself had been short, and, though the United States gave loyal aid to the Allies, when the fighting ended, a considerable amount of group antagonism to the British, French, and Russians asserted itself. The quarrelsome processes of peacemaking at Paris offended a multitude of observers. Critics noted that secret diplomacy promptly reappeared, that some European nations were all too greedy for spoils, and that the idealism which Wilson represented found little response. To many Americans, especially those of German stock, the final peace treaties seemed much too harsh; to many others, typified by Senator Lodge, they seemed much too lenient.

Then, too, the treaty issue was certain to become entangled in politics. Wilson had made a grave tactical error when, just before the armistice, provoked by the harsh attacks of Roosevelt he appealed for a Democratic Congress; and he made another blunder when he failed to include any important Republican leader in the delegation of four (Secretary Lansing, Tasker H. Bliss, E. M. House, and Henry White) , whom he took to the Paris Conference.

Beyond question Wilson's eloquent appeals to American generosity of spirit and to the widespread conviction that "this agony must not be gone through with again" rallied a strong popular majority in 1918–19 to the general project of the League. The House of Representatives, the American Federation of Labor, most church bodies, and many other organizations went on record for it. But Henry Cabot Lodge and other opponents used ingenious means to whittle away part of this majority. They appealed to the rancor of dissatisfied German-Americans, Irish-Americans, and Italian-Americans. They argued that the peace treaty should have been made first and the League established afterward. They criticized the League Covenant in detail. In particular, they sharply attacked Article Ten, which they described as an attempt to freeze the existing political structure of the world and as a move toward a superstate. Their method of delay, dilution, and amendment would have been legitimate had it looked only toward a modification of the Covenant; but William E. Borah, Hiram Johnson, and other bitter-enders were content with nothing less than total defeat. Despite their desperate labors, the President might have won his Senate battle had he retained his physical strength. His gallant speechmaking tour of the country in the summer of 1919 produced a marked effect on public sentiment.

Unfortunately, a paralytic stroke made it necessary for Wilson to break off his tour abruptly at Pueblo, Colorado, and another suffered soon afterward in the White House left him shattered. Lying ill, he was kept badly informed by his wife and physician. Lodge, filled with personal and political animus, made the most of his opportunity; and the

President, taking a stand on principle, committed the error of refusing to compromise on the series of fifteen reservations imposed by the Foreign Relations Committee. On the crucial test (March 20, 1920) a change of seven votes would have carried the treaty. Irreconcilable isolationists and devoted Wilson Democrats stood together against the amended Covenant. Had the President accepted a moderate set of reservations, as Colonel House among others desired, foreign nations would unquestionably have assented. Many thought that he should have done so; others thought that, if he had taken moderate reservations, additional changes would promptly have been added to make sure of the death of the treaty.

As the issue thus went into the campaign of 1920, Republican leaders astutely appealed to all the discontent, weariness, and prejudice which the war had bred. The United States was disengaging itself from the most tremendous effort in its history. It had raised armies of three and a half million soldiers and had flung almost two millions across the Atlantic for battle. It had deployed a navy second only to Britain's, manned by half a million sailors. It had strained its economy to pour out munitions for its own forces and those of the Allies; it had fought a grim battle of fuel at home; and it was still fighting a battle of food, with starvation or succour for millions in Europe and Asia hanging on the issue. By bond drives and heavy taxation it had met war costs, aggregating nearly thirty-seven billion dollars, of which nine and a half billions went in loans to the Allied nations. It had accepted unprecedented constraints upon its economic life, public opinion, and civil liberties. In short, it had come through three years of convulsive exertion, harsh discipline, and searing anxieties—years of enthusiasms and exaltations, but also of losses, hardships, and disillusionments. The cost of living had risen to heights which ordinary folk found distressing, and the economic future was blackly uncertain.

Actually, the popular discontent so realistically exploited by the Republicans had less real basis than many supposed; for Americans who looked realistically at the situation were conscious that their national vigor was untouched, their manpower undepleted, their optimism unquenched. The country's war expenditures had been partly financed out of the prosperity created by heavy European buying in 1914–17. The lessons learned in industrial mobilization were enormously valuable, for men had set up new industries, chemical, automotive, and electrical, that were to prove mines of wealth. The fifty thousand young men killed in action constituted but a light toll, smaller than that annually taken by various forms of accident. By contrast, Americans gazed out on a world horribly devastated and weakened by the conflict. The European powers had lost more than ten million men in battle—France alone one and a third million, the British Empire nine hundred thousand. Great parts of France, Belgium, Serbia, Poland, and Russia had been turned into a blood-stained desert. Elsewhere the destruction of shipping, communications, and buildings had been appalling. Combining direct and indirect losses, the whole cost of the war was later estimated at $370,000,-000,000; and these costs were heavily augmented by the enduring dislocations of economic life. Germany and Russia were too terribly crippled to recover energy for years to come; Britain, France, and Italy were half exhausted; and the six new states which appeared in Europe—Poland, Czechoslovakia, Finland, Lithuania, Latvia, and Esthonia —were trembling with weakness. Compared with the Old World, America was an erect and vigorous giant.

Nevertheless, resentments and fears rather than calm logic dominated the campaign of 1920. The idea that it would provide a solemn referendum upon the League proved a delusion. What took place was essentially a reconstruction election, and the American people instinctively turned (as they had nearly done in 1868) from the party of the war to the party associated with peace. The country was in a state of economic and social flux; questions of prices, wages, markets, employment, and general stability all gravely worried the voters; and problems of domestic readjustment took easy precedence over world affairs. In this situation a multiplicity of irritations did much to sway the electorate. They were irritated by big business, by labor demands, by the heavy recent shifts of population, by incessant shortages in housing, clothing, and food, by foreign turmoil, and by the very idealism of the President—his "preachments." The League issue counted for something, but no man could say just what.

Both parties, but particularly the Republicans, were sharply divided upon the League issue. In the Democratic ranks a small minority wanted no League at all, and a much larger body, while supporting the League, wished to make some concessions to the demand for moderate reservations. William Jennings Bryan had said at a Jackson Day dinner in 1920 that the party could not successfully ask for the rejection of all amendments. In the convention the Administration forces had carried the day, however, with a stiff platform written under Carter Glass's supervision. "We advocate the immediate ratification of the Treaty without reservations which would impair its essential integrity," ran the plank. James M. Cox, nominated as a Middle Westerner not identified with the Administration, courageously made that plank the basic theme of his speeches. So did Franklin D. Roosevelt, the Vice-Presidential nominee, who at the convention had scuffled with Tammany delegates to raise the New York banner in an enthusiastic endorsement of the Wilsonian appeal to the country.

But while the Democratic party successfully closed its ranks, a deeper division in the Republican party had compelled it to straddle the issue. A powerful group of leaders, nearly all Easterners— Taft, Root, Stimson, Wickersham, Nicholas Murray Butler, Hughes—stood for the League with moderate reservations; and so did an influential cohort of party newspapers, led by the New York *Tribune*. Herbert Hoover, his popular prestige at its height, believed in the League principles. Against these men, vindictive haters of Wilson battled so fiercely in the Republican convention that they forced a meaningless compromise. When the Platform Committee produced a plank calling for ratification, Senators Medill McCormick, William E. Borah, and Frank Brandegee denounced it, while Lodge asserted that he would take the floor if necessary to battle it to the finish. The upshot was the adoption of a straddling resolution prepared several weeks earlier by Elihu Root. After condemning the Covenant, the resolution declared that the party "stands for agreement among the nations to preserve the peace of the world"; that "such an international association must . . . maintain the rule of public right by the development of law and the decision of impartial courts"; and that it should "secure instant and general international conference whenever peace shall be threatened by political action so that the nations pledged to do and insist upon whatever is just and fair may exercise their influence and power for the prevention of war." But this concession to the internationalists, unhappily, was balanced by another to the isolationists. All these objects can be achieved, Root's plank stated, "without depriving the people of the United States in advance of the right to determine for themselves what is just and fair when the occasion arises, and without involving them as participants and not as peacemakers in a multitude of quarrels."

The Republican campaign remained equivocal to the end. Warren G. Harding, the mediocre and ignorant candidate nominated with the aid of a Senatorial cabal, made speeches which suggested not so much that he wished to obfuscate the voters' minds as that he had not clarified his own. He spoke of erecting a new tribunal similar to that at The Hague, and of borrowing from the proposed World Court any sound ideas applicable to it. He would even take from the League itself "all that is good and excise all that is bad." Thus, he declared, "we may still have a remnant of world aspirations in 1918 builded into the world's highest conception of useful cooperation." Yet in another speech he flatly asserted that "it is not interpretation but rejection I am seeking." He said later still that he wanted a rational substitute for the League, "or an amended form of it." What he really desired was probably a mystery to himself. Handsome, amiable, shallow, and in everything outside politics and business abysmally uninformed, he had never thought any subject through with tough-minded intensity, and lacked knowledge and ideas to grapple with this one. Throughout the campaign the Borah–Johnson–Brandegee isolationists insisted that the Republicans, if victorious, would turn their backs on world organization. Ex-President Taft, Elihu Root, Charles E. Hughes, Herbert Hoover, and Nicholas Murray Butler, hoping to commit Harding to the League, meanwhile maintained that Republican success would facilitate American entry; and they headed a group of thirty-one prominent men who in October signed an appeal to the voters on this basis.

The unhappiest feature of the campaign was its fierce evocation of prejudices, fears, and antipathies. The resentments of many German-Americans who detested the peace of Versailles, of Italian-Americans who thought that Italy should have received Fiume, of Irish-Americans who supported DeValera, and of other hyphenated groups, were stirred in a seething cauldron. Slogans were given a currency which kept them potent for years to come: no entangling alliances; no foreign snares; no more sacrifice of American boys in foreign wars; no impairment of sovereignty. Many journals and speakers tried to create the totally false impression that the costly conflict just ended had not really been an American conflict, and that the republic had been used and victimized by the Allied powers. The idea was adroitly emphasized that the United States ought always to take an attitude of suspicion toward the Old World; and Washington's Farewell Address and the Monroe Doctrine were deliberately misconstrued as evidence that the nation's early leaders had wished to keep it aloof from the rest of the globe.

The campaign thus left a long-felt legacy of prejudice. Even so-called liberal organs like the *Nation* joined in the hue and cry against Britain and France. Altogether, the years 1919–20 created a political miasma which no sun of reasonableness could pierce, and left much of the country befogged by notions which better suited the eighteenth than the twentieth century. Isolationist leaders, with a variety of demagogues both political and literary, thereafter labored to keep the widespread mistrusts of Europe alive. The fact that it proved difficult to organize peace in the Old World, and that Ireland, Egypt, Upper Silesia, Danzig, and Syria were for some time centers of unrest and violence, made it easier to give impatient Americans a dislike of the whole foreign scene.

Till five months after his triumphant election, Harding kept the world uncertain of his course in dealing with the League. He conferred with both advocates and antagonists of American entry. Taft, Hoover, Hughes, Oscar S. Straus, and Porter J. McCumber (the one Republican who had voted for ratification without reservations) talked with him. So did Lodge, Borah, Brandegee, McCormick, and James E. Watson. The selection of the Cabinet did not resolve the puzzle. Thrusting aside the ambitious Albert B. Fall, the President made Charles E. Hughes—one-time governor of New York, member of the Supreme Court, and in 1916 Presidential candidate, an able, broadly educated, and circumspect man—his Secretary of State. Hughes's whole career was indicative of keen analytical power, high integrity, and judicial balance; he believed in the principle of internationalism, but he was not a man who would fight hard enough for it to make rough enemies. He was urbanely, rather than aggressively, in favor of the League. Hoover, a fervent believer in world cooperation, was made Secretary of Commerce. Meanwhile, Andrew W. Mellon, who had helped to finance the anti-League battle, became Secretary of the Treasury; Fall, the double-distilled isolationism of the Far West in his veins, took the

Interior Department; and John W. Weeks, a Bay State conservative close to the vindictive Lodge, was appointed Secretary of War. Obviously, the Cabinet was divided on the League issue.

Even in his inaugural address Harding still carried water on both shoulders. On the one hand he said: "America can be a party to no permanent military alliance. It can make no political commitments." On the other he declared: "We have no thought to impede the paths to closer relationship. We wish to promote understanding. We want to do our part in making offensive warfare so hateful that governments and peoples who resort to it must prove the righteousness of their cause or stand as outlaws before the bar of civilization." Seizing upon these bland phrases, the London *Spectator* (and some Americans) fatuously hoped to the end for acceptance of the Covenant.

The best-informed comment following Harding's election, however, always predicted that he would renounce the League. His closest associates, George Harvey, Richard Washburn Child, Senator James Watson of Indiana, and others like them, were fierce in antagonism to the Covenant. To Borah, Boies Penrose, and other anti-League Senators, Harding chiefly owed his nomination. Considerations of party unity weighed heavily with him; and while the implacable Lodge–Borah–Brandegee cabal could make or mar his Administration, no internationalists possessed the force to do so. His ignorance of world needs was profound. It was natural that he should drift into an isolationist interpretation of the election. "You just didn't want a surrender of the United States of America," he had told his Marion neighbors; "you wanted America to go on under American ideals. That's why you didn't care for the League which is now deceased." He soon reinterpreted his campaign utterances. Forgetting that his statements had been distinctly equivocal, and ignoring the uncontradicted manifesto of the thirty-one leading Republicans, he spoke just after inauguration of party *pledges* to repudiate the League. "In compliance with its pledges," he told the Associated Press, "the new Administration which came into power in March, 1921, definitely and decisively put aside all thoughts of entering the League of Nations. It doesn't propose to enter now, by the side door, back door, or cellar door."

Was the League "deceased"? Events quickly proved that it was not. For fifty nations it was soon a living, useful, hopeful organization. The Harding Administration, finding that it could not treat the League as nonexistent, had to determine whether its attitude should be cooperative and helpful, or hostile and obstructive. Absolute neutrality was impossible.

Two diverse worlds, one of reality and one of

theory, at once came into conflict. The reality was
the constant shrinkage of the globe under pressure
of modern communications—the airplane, radio,
cable, telephone—until Europe and America were
closer by 1935 than Boston and New York had
been a century earlier. The growing economic interdependence of nations, so intimate that industries
of Michigan and Ohio found profit or ruin in the
marketing arrangements of Malaysian rubber-grow-
ers and the seesaw of militarist and pacifist parties
in Japan; the financial unity of the world, which
made American banking reel under the failure of
the Kredit-Anstalt in Austria; and the indivisibility
of peace, as the Russian statesman Litvinov soon
phrased it, meant that war anywhere, in Spain or
Ethiopia, affected peace-loving peoples everywhere.

The theoretical world built up by the wide diffusion of hate and suspicion in 1920 was very different. It was a world dominated, in George Wickersham's words, by "the hampering influence upon
government of prejudices against international
agreements of any kind, the popular belief that a
nation can live unto itself and yet share in prosperous foreign commerce with others, the delusion
that war can be prevented by mere declarations of
'outlawry.'" In the end, the world of reality was
fated to destroy the world of distorted theory—but
the process had to be long and painful.

A still deeper antithesis grew out of the Senate

debate and the Presidential campaign; an antithesis which lent immeasurably greater significance to the conflict between two worlds, one dead and the other struggling to be born. The United States, misled by the sweeping isolationist clamor against Europe, failed to comprehend the necessity for a continuing interest in the struggle between democracy and autocracy. President Wilson and the co-founders of the League, Taft, James Bryce, Sir Edward Grey, Jan Smuts, Aristide Briand, and others, believed that the advanced peace-loving nations must unite in making the world safe for democracy. They knew that countries which were compelled by a constant state of fear to arm to the teeth, to keep themselves momentarily ready for war, and to maintain a high degree of economic self-sufficiency, must decline from democracy toward autocracy. Democracy thus had a vital stake in collective security. Just after 1919–20, the great British and French democracies were almost as bitterly denounced in America as Imperial Germany had been. This was both absurd and disastrous. If the United States had joined the League, it would necessarily have recognized its fundamental political kinship with the British and French peoples. It might then have played a larger and more active role in fostering the Weimar Republic; and it would probably not have remained indifferent to the rise of fascism in Italy.

In time the growth of totalitarian dogmas and the

emergence of one brutal dictator after another generated a sharp conflict between the old-style democracies like Britain and France and the new-style autocracies like Germany and Japan. To many observers the democratic group seemed timid and feeble, the totalitarian states dynamic and lusty. In this conflict the United States, under the spell of the cynicism generated in the League battle, tried too long to remain neutral. Its attitude seemed for a time plausible. Then as the ideological warfare grew pitiless, its position became untenable, destroyed by the march of events.

For a variety of reasons the Republican Administration after 1921 yielded to the nationalist ideas which, in combination with *laissez-faire* economics, were shaping a materialistic and reactionary era. Even Secretary Hughes bowed to party loyalty; in 1922, speaking for Lodge's reelection in Massachusetts, he expressed scorn for the thought that the American people would ever consent "to assume any obligations, moral or legal, which would fetter their appropriate freedom of action in unknown contingencies." Many Republicans, including a majority of the Senate Foreign Relations Committee, disliked Wilson and his ideas so intensely that they actually hoped for a quick dissolution of the League. Numerous isolationists even convinced themselves that loyalty to the League was akin to treason, and tolerance of it un-American. Some

Congressional leaders, fearing that the United States might be gradually seduced into such close association that League membership would follow, held total avoidance the only safety. The numerous European and Asiatic broils which accompanied the readjustments of peace convinced others that America was well out of such a melee. Bitter, ungenerous, vindictive—such had been the diehard opposition to Wilson and the Covenant; and ungenerous remained the attitude of many Republicans toward the great world organization. Total isolation was of course impossible to the United States, for its interests were world-wide; but political isolation from the Old World was combined with a strong promotion of economic expansion overseas.

For the first time in history, a true parliament of nations began its sittings. The League Assembly, convoked by Wilson, met immediately after Harding's election. Forty-two nations were represented in that first Assembly, while fourteen others applied for entry, of which six were admitted. Canada had joined along with the other members of the British Commonwealth; all of the Latin-American countries which were invited to enter had accepted. The five European neutrals in the late conflict hastened to support the organization, all enthusiastically. In Sweden and Switzerland, to be sure, a few people were offended by the exclusion of Germany, while others feared a loss of their traditional neutrality; yet the Swedish Parliament voted two to one for entry, and the Swiss plebiscite was decisive. The initial debates proved that the Assembly might become a true world forum. Its President, Paul Hymans of Belgium, held sway with impartiality, while the delegates included such able men as Lord Robert Cecil of England, Benes of Czechoslovakia, Nansen of Norway, Branting of Sweden, and Motta of Switzerland. Later in 1921 a second Assembly session admitted the four new Baltic republics.

The League Council had meanwhile been holding a notable series of gatherings. The first took place in Paris early in 1920, and ten more followed that year. Steps were taken to prevent war between Poland and Lithuania over Vilna, and to reconcile the Swedes and Finns, quarreling over the Aland Islands; a Mandates Commission was set up; commissioners were named to administer the Saar Valley and Danzig; and jurists were empaneled to write the constitution of the Permanent Court of International Justice.

While the United States had officially turned its back on this high endeavor, great numbers of Americans viewed it with warm sympathy; and as the League thus took on strength, Secretary Hughes had to formulate a related American policy. He could not act as if the United States was a member, nor as if the Harding Administration hoped for

its success. To decide upon a method of dealing with
its requests, and to hammer out a protocol for
negotiating, would take considerable thought and
time. Hughes, preoccupied with urgent duties, left
the matter to subordinates, who simply pigeon-
holed the first League communications. The Wilson
Administration had answered or at least acknowledged fifteen missives from the League, leaving
eighteen still to be considered. When Hughes be-
latedly learned that correspondence had accumulated without action, he ordered a response. The
unfortunate fact was that not until September 22,
1921, did the State Department vouchsafe any
response to League notes, and it then followed the
usual formula in treating with unrecognized governments—that is, letters were written in the third per-
son, were not signed, and instead of being sent
directly to the Secretary-General (Sir Eric Drummond) were delivered by the Swiss Legation or the
Geneva Consul. The American policy was in effect
non-recognition.

In instance after instance the frigid American
policy inconvenienced other countries and hampered the nascent League. Since problems of international health, made urgent by post-war confusion
and exhaustion, demanded efficient treatment, a
Health Committee of the League was set up, with a
Health Section in the Secretariat. Most of the
world's leading agencies for the promotion of pub-

lic health approved the step. American medical
officers who had carried on Red Cross work in
Europe warmly supported it. But the State Department, refusing to recognize the new body, insisted
upon working with an inadequate Office International d'Hygiéne Publique which had carried on a
creaky existence in Paris since 1907 and which other
countries were now ready to jettison. The world
therefore found it necessary to maintain two international health organizations. Similarly, Washington declined to act with the League in controlling
the narcotics traffic. While other nations transferred
important undertakings to the League's Opium
Committee, the United States for some time refused even to furnish information to this body except through the roundabout medium of the Dutch
Government.

Even in the creation of the Permanent Court of
International Justice, popularly called the World
Court, Washington in its stiff spirit of nationalism
created unfortunate obstacles. That Court made a
peculiar appeal to many Americans. The United
States had taken a deep interest in the Hague Arbitration Tribunal, on which Elihu Root, Oscar
Straus, John Bassett Moore, and George Gray had
held places. The new agency possessed broader
powers, for it was to determine any dispute of an
international character which the parties thereto
might submit, and to give an advisory opinion upon

any quarrel referred to it by the Council or Assembly. Experts believed that, sitting continuously and interpreting international law, it would become a tribunal of supreme usefulness. The Council moved promptly to create the Court, appointing in February, 1920, a committee of jurists to draft its basic statute; and with President Wilson's approval, Root accepted a place on this committee. At Root's suggestion, the statute provided that the Assembly and Council should elect members of the Court from lists submitted by the Hague Tribunal judges. In due course the Secretary-General of the League asked the four American judges to submit nominations. They would have done so had not Secretary Hughes, when consulted, objected that they would be acting under a treaty to which the United States was not a party. The election was therefore held without American assistance.

Still other instances of American chilliness toward the League might be named. It would be unfair to say that they all sprang from a fear of offending the powerful isolationist block in the Senate, of stultifying the Republican declarations of policy, of somehow losing votes among the Anglophobes, Francophobes, and Russophobes, and of giving the Democratic party an advantage which they might exploit. They reflected these fears, but they also reflected the political immaturity of the American people and the natural public revulsion from the spectacle of Old World confusion and rivalry. There were similar expressions of nationalism in various other lands.

It was soon clear, however, that the League was in no sense whatever the "superstate" Harding had disdainfully mentioned. It had no armed forces, no power of taxation, no sovereign authority. Its main defect was weakness, not excess of strength. It was soon also plain that the League was not destined to an early death, or indeed to any death without a powerful successor. Its membership later reached a peak roll of sixty nations. At one time or another its roster included every great power except the United States, and every small country except Arabia. Its gatherings at Geneva, attended by many of the world's leading statesmen, opened a bright new chapter in human affairs.

The dispute between Finland and Sweden over the Aland Islands was settled by the Council in June, 1921; Finland gained possession of the islands, but gave Sweden guarantees that they would be neutralized, would never be fortified, and would offer Swedish residents certain rights through an autonomous statute. In dealing with the Polish-Lithuanian dispute over Vilna, the Council in 1920–21 succeeded in averting war, although it failed to effect a permanent settlement. The League healed another dangerous sore when in the spring of 1921 it took up the Polish-German dispute over

Upper Silesia, which had become so grave that an explosion was momentarily feared. The Council saw to it that, following a plebiscite, the area was partitioned with reasonable equity, while it required each nation to sign a convention for the protection of minorities left under its jurisdiction. A little later, in 1923, a dramatic collision occurred between Greece and Italy, when, following the murder of some boundary commissioners, Italian forces occupied the island of Corfu. Italy ranked as a great power and was a member of the Council. Yet that body showed a determination to see the controversy settled justly and without force. In the end it was the Council of Ambassadors which obtained Italy's withdrawal, but the firm attitude of the League Council had meanwhile evoked general commendation.

In still other respects the League showed a growing vigor. It helped adjust various boundaries in eastern Europe, lent a hand in solving the Memel problem, and assisted Albania to a position of stability. Year by year it encouraged arbitration and conciliation, preparing model treaties for nations which wished to adopt these methods. Its Secretariat was busy disseminating information on international affairs. In the social and humanitarian sphere, its work in caring for refugees, fighting epidemics, promoting public health, limiting the sale of narcotics, and protecting women and children commanded equal admiration. No reasonable man could deny that American participation in such League activities would have redounded to the credit of the republic.

As the years passed, the old uneasiness lest the United States should somehow be tricked into the League disappeared, and a belief in its beneficent possibilities for the world at large gained ground. Non-recognition therefore soon gave way to recognition—and limited assistance. Early in 1923 President Harding informed the Senate that he had no "unseemly" (he meant "ungracious") comment to offer on the League. "If it is serving the Old World helpfully, more power to it. But it is not for us." Later that year President Coolidge reaffirmed this policy. The country, he declared in his annual message, had definitely rejected the Covenant, and he would propose no change in policy. "The incident, so far as we are concerned, is closed. The League exists as a foreign agency." But Coolidge had at one time favored joining the League, and he now indicated no hostility toward it.

When Republican Presidents could speak of the League without objurgation or contempt, their Secretaries of State could take advantage of its conveniences for international action. A negative attitude was as hurtful to the United States as it was to the world. The first step to meet the necessities of the situation was the appointment of "unoffi-

cial observers" to share in the discussions of non-
political agencies of the League. The initial nomination was that of Grace Abbott in October, 1922, "to
cooperate in an unofficial and consultative capacity" with the League's advisory committee on the
traffic in women and children. Soon afterward unofficial observers were appointed to sessions of an
anthrax committee and of the advisory committee
on opium traffic. The Government decided to cooperate with the League's health committee after
all. When the election of a new member of the
World Court took place, no impediment was placed
in the way of American nominations. The year
1927 found the United States accepting every invitation but one which it received from Geneva, and
that one pertained purely to political matters.

By that date, indeed, Americans agreed that their
Government could properly assist in all social, economic, humanitarian, and scientific undertakings.
When the League took up the issue of double taxation, the United States (after one refusal) found
it profitable to participate. When in 1927 Geneva
convoked an International Economic Conference,
an able American delegation, its expenses paid by
Congress, was present. In dealing with international control of private traffic in armaments, the
United States at first declined to have anything to
do with the League's efforts to draft an effective
convention; and it maintained this position as late

as September, 1923, when the State Department addressed a stiff note on the subject to the League Council. But before long the Government decided to have its Minister in Switzerland sit with a temporary mixed commission in drafting a new convention, and, though he explained that his duty was simply to "receive information," he was soon sharing in the discussions. In 1925 the United States sent delegates under Representative Burton of Ohio to a diplomatic conference considering the draft convention; and they shared the debate, carried a separate agreement on poison gas, and signed the two resulting treaties.

The weaknesses of the League, as time proved, were many and radical. Yet had the United States become a member, its power combined with that of Britain and France *might* have given the organization the ultimate force which was indispensable. As more than one student has pointed out, a virtual concert between American and British sea power had, with brief though important interruptions, been tacitly accepted for more than a century; or if concert is too strong a word, a remarkable degree of mutual trust had existed. Upon that quasi-entente of the two greatest Atlantic powers the League could have relied for its main authority. France would have been the third party in the nuclear group, asserting views of its own and modifying the positions of the two Anglo-Saxon states.

These three nations could have guaranteed the immediate future of the world. Wilson has been reproached for failing to discern the absolute necessity for such an alliance. The reproach falls rather upon his opponents, for the great war President would have accepted the reality without the name, while the xenophobes of the Senate tolerated neither.

After the defection of America, the League fell back upon the collective authority of some fifty states, with a precarious entente between Britain and France as its chief pillar. Undoubtedly, Wilson, Cecil, and other idealists had greatly exaggerated the potentialities of an association of second-rank and third-rank nations, mistakenly believing that partial union would give them strength. Time showed that the small nations nearly always waited to see what the great powers would do, and that invariably the action of the great powers was decisive. Wilson and his associates likewise exaggerated the possibility of maintaining peace by mere economic pressure. Again time proved that unless economic pressure was backed by a firm show of armed force, it was worthless, for any nation subjected to the threat of industrial prostration would fight.

In their retrospect upon the events of 1918–25, Americans later divided into two main schools: one argued that had the United States joined the collective security system, Geneva could have kept the

world lapped in law and thus have prevented the
terrible catastrophe which occurred twenty years
later; the other school asserted that whether America had joined or not, the jealousies and greeds of
the Old World would have wrecked the League.
The first school quoted Wilson's eloquent prediction of the Second World War. He spoke prophet-
ically when in 1924, stigmatizing "selfish isolation"
as "deeply ignoble," he declared: "We shall inevitably be forced by the moral obligations of freedom
and honor to retrieve that fatal error and assume
once more the role of courage, self-respect, and help-
fulness which every true American must wish and
believe to be our true part in world affairs." Members of this first school could show how near the
League *did* come to a spectacular success, how small
was the margin by which the avalanche began to
slip. Had the League in 1931 been strong enough to
intervene powerfully against Japan in Manchuria,
such action might well have deterred Hitler and
Mussolini from their subsequent forays. As late as
1936, had the League been able to take effective
steps to halt Mussolini's invasion of Ethiopia, the
whole tragic lurch toward world conflict might have
been stopped. No such cogent arguments can be
offered by those who believe that Geneva would
have failed even had America lent it a vigorous
leadership.

But the question cannot be rightly understood

unless we see the League aright. The United States would not really have been joining a collective-security union of fifty-odd nations; essentially, it would have been joining an alliance of a few powers loosely supported by fifty lesser countries. Upon Britain, France, and the United States, augmented later by Russia and a half-unified China, would have fallen the main burden of maintaining peace. Could American sentiment have reconciled itself to the compromises requisite in maintaining an alliance of three or five powers? Would such an alliance have proved efficient? If the answer is yes, the American people made one of the greatest errors of their history when in 1919–21 they turned their backs on the League. After fighting the war for democratic security and world peace, they had thrown away their victory.

At no time did one strong section of American opinion lose faith in the League idea, and at all times the League accomplished a great deal in indoctrinating Americans with its best aims. The fruits of that indoctrination were ultimately to appear. In the spring of 1946, with the battle smoke slowly lifting from three continents, the League Assembly held in Geneva its final meeting. Of the original architects only one, Lord Robert Cecil, was present. The great British idealist, then in his eighty-second year, had sacrificed office and power for the sake of the international experiment. To the

extent that the League had failed, he said in his
valedictory speech, it was because the current of
official opinion in all major nations had been indifferent or hostile to the idea of collective security.
But in a larger sense it had not failed, for it had
laid the foundation for a stronger and far more
hopeful body, the United Nations. Of that new
body the United States, its last shreds of isolationism discarded, was a leading member and a determined supporter. It had been slow in learning that
Woodrow Wilson was right, but it had learned.

CHAPTER III

"WE have two courses in the United States," Secretary Hughes told a London audience on July 21, 1924. "We can enter upon a field of controversy involving our historic traditions, the fears and hopes of racial groups, and accomplish nothing. We can frankly recognize the sphere of action we can usefully fill, and accomplish much." As this statement implied, Hughes thought it wise to avoid reopening the heated controversies of 1918–21, to leave the development of the League to Europe, and to use American influence in ways that were conservative and safe. Himself a man of high ideals as well as great ability, he was assisted by veterans in the State Department who were equally anxious to help the world out of its terrible confusion. His first Under-Secretary of State was Henry P. Fletcher, a onetime Rough Rider who had been Ambassador to Chile and Mexico under Wilson. In 1922 another capable career officer, William Phillips, became Under-Secretary, and in 1924 a third, Joseph C.

Grew. The First Assistant Secretary when Hughes took office was Fred M. Dearing, while the Second Assistant Secretary was the deaf, witty, and resourceful Alvah A. Adee, who had been active in the Department since 1882, and who had become a walking encyclopedia of diplomatic history and protocol. His death in 1924 was a severe loss.

Resolved to do as much as possible for world order within the non-controversial limits he had marked out, Hughes handled his larger relationships with tact and skill. He maintained cordial contacts with peppery Senator Lodge of the Senate Foreign Relations Committee, and with Oscar Underwood, leading Democratic member of that body. His own foreign appointments were wisely made. He suffered much from Harding's blunder in appointing George Harvey as Ambassador to Great Britain, where the bad manners, bad personal habits, and loose talk of that isolationist envoy did great harm. Harding sent an equally weak representative, Richard Washburn Child, to Italy. Fortunately, the experienced and popular Myron T. Herrick remained in Paris. Hughes and his aides labored steadily to improve the foreign service; and in Latin America, an area in which the Secretary disavowed any imperialistic objects, particularly good men were named.

One token of the new position the United States had reached in world affairs was the passage in

1924 of the Rogers Act for reorganizing the foreign service. For some years Representative John Jacob Rogers of Massachusetts had been urging a reorganization. In 1922, after much consultation with Hughes, he introduced a bill embodying the best of his own ideas and those of Hughes. Public hearings were held, the press gave the bill strong support, and it became law. The consular and diplomatic services were amalgamated as the foreign service of the United States, in nine grades on a strict merit basis, with regular promotion; salaries were increased, and recruitment and retirement systems established; consular and diplomatic officers were made interchangeable, while assignments to home service in the State Department were put on a systematic footing. Although the act did not apply to heads of missions, the President in his executive order putting it into effect suggested that service men should be promoted to the higher posts, and this was soon done. The United States was still free to appoint such distinguished men as Bancroft and Lowell, Hay and Choate, to its best diplomatic positions, but in practice all but a few embassies came to be filled, in the next twenty years, by career men. The service profited.

Had Hughes been free to consider merely ordinary diplomatic problems, the highly creditable record that he made in that field would have shone forth with lustre. Unfortunately, the most pressing

problems after the war were economic problems and
hence largely outside his control. John Maynard
Keynes had remarked in his *Economic Consequences of the Peace* (1920) that the outlook was
one of pessimism. The peace treaty, he said, included no provision for the economic rehabilitation
of Europe, none for the restoration of the disordered
finances of France and Italy, none for the promotion of economic solidarity among the Allies themselves, and none "to adjust the systems of the Old
World and the New." This adjustment between
America and the Old World was destined to be a
painful process.

The modern world is primarily a business world,
and its degree of political stability must always be
closely connected with its economic stability. All
nations think of the dollar, the pound, the franc,
the mark. These are symbols of plenty or want.
When the First World War ended, the most exigent
problems were the provision of food, clothing, buildings, seed, and machinery; that is, the business
problems. Any economist could have predicted that
the chief nations involved in the war would have to
pass through three difficult phases of readjustment.
The first would be a brief period in which they
shifted from war to civilian production, with many
shortages, high prices, and a considerable amount
of unemployment while industries "tooled up." The
second would be a longer period of catching up with

consumer demand; of high employment while surplus savings were spent, long-postponed purchases were made, and supplies of goods were increased to match new rises in income. The third period, and the most troublesome, would represent a transition from the catching-up phase to a stable and balanced economy. It would profit all nations, and particularly the United States as the greatest power, to take a long-run view of general world interests rather than a short-term view of purely selfish national interests.

Unhappily, the strong political nationalism which marked the course of the United States under Harding, Coolidge, and Hoover drew much of its strength from economic nationalism. American business wanted to paddle its own canoe toward the nearest dollars. Uncle Sam resolved to look after his own pocket alone. Legislation on tariffs, war debts, and other subjects was directed toward immediate American interests without much regard to world welfare. Most manufacturing and trading groups in American upheld this policy. To be sure, the historic low-tariff groups and certain other liberal elements opposed it. Not a few Americans sympathized with the foreigner who, asked on entering New York harbor what he thought of the skyscrapers, replied: "They remind me of your tariffs!" Such men battled in vain. Secretary Hughes had little to do with the general economic policy, and its direction obviously troubled him, as later it troubled his successors, Kellogg and, above all, Stimson. President Harding, Secretary Mellon, and Republican members of Congress, representing for the most part the big business that took control after the war, dealt with commercial and financial policies.

Big business did expect the State Department to help look after its investments. In this area of policy Hughes took a much more moderate course than his last Republican predecessor, Philander C. Knox. The Wilson Administration had refused to recognize the Obregón regime in Mexico because it would not give satisfactory assurances that, under the Constitution of 1917, American mining and ranching rights would be respected. Hughes continued this policy while laboring for a settlement. In 1923 an agreement was worked out: Mexico gave pledges that American property acquired before 1917 would not be confiscated; and diplomatic relations were resumed.

Of the Republican leaders of big business outlook, Andrew F. Mellon, who remained in the Cabinet after Coolidge became President, best typified the economic nationalism of the time. About the silent, elegant figure of the Secretary of the Treasury, one of the world's richest men, who wore an ascetic face of a dreamer and mystic, grew up a luxuriant myth. Although he had amassed a vast fortune in banking and in aluminum manufacture and had col-

lected a fabulous body of paintings, he was almost
unknown when he left Pittsburgh for Washington.
To some, in the ensuing years he became the greatest public financier since Hamilton. He balanced
the budget; he greatly reduced tax burdens; he persuaded reluctant European debtors to pay their
dues to Uncle Sam. Others held with Walter Lippmann that Mellon's resemblance to Hamilton began
and ended with the fact that both men believed
that the nation's salvation lay in government by
the rich. The war-debts settlement, these critics intimated, had been shortsightedly harsh, and the
tariffs were harsher still. Yet despite all carpings,
so long as the good times lasted Secretary Mellon
typified policies which most Americans apparently
applauded.

In the years preceding the war, an ever-growing
degree of world prosperity had been built upon a
close trade relationship among a great variety of
nations dealing in a complex multiplicity of products. Some countries were heavily industrialized,
some were wholly agricultural, and others possessed
varying stages of a mixed economy. The value of
goods shipped in international channels had increased from $17,800,000,000 in 1890 to $39,200,-
000,000 in 1912. A merchant marine of more than
45,000,000 gross tons was required in 1914 to carry
this traffic. Of the world's trade, Great Britain (exclusive of her colonies) had 16.6 per cent in 1912;

Germany had 12.9 per cent; the United States 9.9 per cent; and France 9 per cent. A banking and credit system which, on the whole, possessed remarkable stability and security, had met the demands of the commercial world. All the major Occidental powers had possessed a gold-based currency; in all of them, this currency fluctuated within narrow limits. Capital flowed freely from nation to nation, restricted for the most part only by laws of investment risk.

This delicate and yet powerful mechanism had been disrupted by the conflict. Devastation, impoverishment, and an abnormal distortion of the economic structure characterized large parts of Europe and Asia. Meanwhile, the United States, the British Dominions, and a few other countries experienced a rapid industrial advance. When the war ended, the world market was contracted, and trade competition grew more intense. International credit lay in ruins, the currency systems of the great nations (even the United States) were terribly shaken, and mountains of debt had to be shouldered. Every wheat-grower and cotton-planter in America felt the loss of European buying power. The gold stocks of the world had been weirdly redistributed, some nations losing nearly all their reserves. At one blow the Communist Revolution had robbed France, Italy, Britain, and other countries of pre-war and wartime loans to Russia aggregating billions. Germany faced a staggering reparations burden, which no one knew whether she could pay.

The two great powers which had emerged from the war with increased strength were Japan and the United States; and the United States stood amid the general chaos like a colossus. The sums due it from the Allies totaled about eleven and a half billions. So much gold had flowed to American shores that the first quarter of 1924 found the republic in possession of nearly half the gold reserves of the globe: $4,385,900,000 out of $9,562,500,000. Between 1913 and 1922 the per capita value of exports by the United States increased 33 per cent, that of French exports by 25 per cent, and that of the United Kingdom exports by 20 per cent.

As the world's greatest creditor nation, the largest producer of agricultural and other raw materials, and incomparably the strongest financial power, the United States held a position which made her economic activities more significant than those of any two other powers combined. President Wilson had hoped that economic internationalism, involving a marked reduction of tariffs and other impediments, would rule the post-war world. In a free flow of goods and services, with an automatic adjustment of national economies, he saw the best likelihood of stability. This wise hope was doomed to disappointment. In the uncertainty of the post-war years, nations demanded government intervention to protect special interests and to manage the national life. Even Great Britain, as her path became more rugged, was converted to protectionism.

For nearly two years after the close of the war the United States enjoyed a prosperity pillared upon large-scale Government spending, a keen demand for consumer's goods, and a heavy flow of wares and food to Europe. It was checked at the close of 1920 by a brief depression. As European nations came to the end of their ready funds and credits, foreign purchases sagged. The export trade had been primarily responsible for American prosperity; its collapse was the chief element in the sudden deflation of prices, wages, and employment. While in 1919 there had been fewer than 6,500 mercantile and industrial failures, in 1921 there were very nearly 20,000. The average hourly wage, as reported by the National Industrial Conference Board, dropped from a peak of 62.1 cents in 1920 to 48.2 cents in December of 1921. Estimates of unemployed during 1921 reached five or six millions.

Even without this temporary depression, a radical revision of the tariff upward was to have been expected. The war and the ensuing Presidential campaign had strengthened the doctrine of "America First." Industries created or heavily stimulated by the conflict clamored for protection and were supported by farmers feeling painfully the end of the war boom. Even before Wilson went out of office an emergency tariff had been laid upon his desk. He vetoed it with a message full of economic wisdom, which deserved far more respect than it got. Above all, wrote Wilson, the new creditor position of the United States required a more statesmanlike policy in dealing with trade. Debtor nations could not pay their obligations if forbidden to ship goods, while the country's long-term wellbeing depended upon steady recovery abroad. "Clearly, this is no time for the erection of high trade barriers," concluded the President.

But with Harding's accession, a special session swiftly passed an emergency tariff which became law on May 27, 1921. It was shortly followed by the more comprehensive Fordney-McCumber Act of September 19, 1922, the highest tariff thus far known in American history. Special attention was paid to such "war babies" as the chemical and dyestuffs industries. Iron and steel duties, omitted from the Underwood Tariff, went back on the statute book. Textile rates were sharply increased. Special schedules were written for agricultural products, though in most categories they would avail the farmer nothing. Altogether, Congress erected a wall across which the foreign producer could sell only with the greatest difficulty.

The high American tariffs were an evil not merely in themselves, but in the example they set European nations. As early as 1926 the growing intensity of international economic warfare aroused widespread uneasiness. In October of that year more than two hundred leading bankers, manufacturers, and merchants of America and Europe issued a ringing manifesto. "There can be no recovery in Europe," they said, "till politicians in all countries, old and new, realize that trade is not war, but a process of exchange, that in time of peace our neighbors are our customers, and that their prosperity is a condition of our own well-being." But the competition in raising barriers went merrily on. Between midsummer of 1926 and the summer of 1930, the countries of Europe, Latin America, and the British Empire carried out fifty-seven major revisions with regard to import trade, of which forty-three were distinctly upward. Fear grew. Antagonism grew with it. A pernicious step toward strait-jacketing European trade was taken when France devised her quota system, which Czechoslovakia and other lands quickly imitated. Six nations distinguished themselves after 1926 by competitive zeal in shutting the doors on home markets, and by the use of very hard and ugly methods to promote foreign trade: the United States, Britain, Japan, France, Germany, and Russia.

The result of the Fordney-McCumber Act was that, although the United States maintained a large export surplus through the 1920's, it did so only by exporting capital on a tremendous scale. For both the United States and the world at large, the years 1922–29 were a period of economic expansion, rising income, and growing world trade. American industry experienced an astonishing boom. Agriculture, however, failed to keep pace with the general prosperity. In a period of sharp world competition and generally falling prices, the farmers were weighed down by wartime debts contracted to increase their production. They were unwilling to lower their output and, as profits failed, they resorted to borrowing in order to tide themselves over. During the years 1920–29, they obtained assistance from the Government and banks which increased their debt by about 20 per cent. They were thus placed in a position where any new contraction in demand and additional fall in prices would mean disaster.

The spectacular export of American capital during the twenties can be summarized in a few striking figures. During 1919–30, the United States sent abroad an annual average of nearly a billion dollars ($965,000,000) through flotation of new foreign loan issues and direct new investments overseas. In the same period, the short-term assets of the United States abroad were increased by a little over a billion. On the other side of the ledger, the offsetting items were comparatively small. Thus amortizations and retirements of foreign debts came to only about $3,300,000,000, while overseas buyers "repatriated" their foreign securities to but a minor extent.

The great boom period in foreign flotations comprised the four years from the middle of 1924 to the middle of 1928. During this flush era, banking interests vied in peddling issues which were often grossly unsafe. They sent agents to sit on the doorsteps and haunt the anterooms of foreign governments, municipal, state, and national; they persuaded some of these governments to borrow more than they really needed; and they then sold the bonds at high interest rates to the American public. In Peru bribery was actually employed to get the Government to take a loan; in that country, Chile, Bolivia, and Germany, the overborrowing was obvious to all; and in Cuba and Peru in particular the proceeds of the loans were spent with shocking wastefulness. Many a rueful American investor, in the end, lost heavily. Direct investments abroad were also lavish. Whether made by corporations whose primary field of operations was the United States, by corporations organized to conduct foreign operations, or by foreign corporations in which Americans took large holdings, they gave other nations a generous supply of dollars. An "expansionist psychology" lay behind many of these investments.

Altogether, the export of capital made the United States by 1929 a net creditor to the world for about twenty-one billion dollars. While considerably more than half of this was represented by intergovernmental debts, the total long-term assets held in private hands came to about nine and a half billions. Meanwhile, the United States (the first major nation to reestablish the gold standard after the war) had augmented its gold holdings, other nations shipping the precious metal across the ocean for badly needed dollar exchange. Hence the year 1929 found America holding about 28 per cent of the world's entire stock of gold.

In their reluctance to balance commodity exports by commodity imports, Americans were actuated by a myopic view of self-interest. The Government pushed foreign shipments with unflagging vigor. Yet it showed quick resentment when any foreign power adopted measures inspired by the grosser forms of economic nationalism. Ruthless competition among producers of raw rubber just after the war forced prices so low that British planters in 1923 adopted the Stevenson Plan for limiting the amounts sent to market. For a time this seemed successful. The price per pound, which had sunk to 27 cents, rose by irregular advances to 95 cents in 1925, and momentarily touched a dollar in the New York market. Secretary Hoover sternly denounced the Stevenson Plan, and expressed the general American exultation when a heavy inflow of competitive supplies from the Dutch East Indies again broke the market. Washington was similarly hostile to the attempt of Anglo-Dutch mining interests to develop a tin cartel, which received some governmental support, including a high British export tax on tin ore. The efforts of Brazil to bolster a weak market for coffee encountered resentful opposition in Washington. Yet the time lay just ahead when the United States, through the AAA and the Bankhead Act, would hold the price of cotton and other farm commodities at an artificial level and by a series of laws would bolster the price of silver to the heavy damage of China, Mexico, and other silver-using nations.

On the whole, the American management of trade and finance during the 1920's left much to be desired. The nation had become a giant in almost all fields of production. Its exports were enormous. Its tariffs largely limited its imports to essential materials, tropical products, and some highly specialized goods. Under these circumstances, an adjustment in the trade balance to permit a return flow of debt-service payments presented great difficulty. It could probably have been accomplished, as the Commerce Department later stated, without grave disturbance to the export structure and the whole internal economy, only if certain steps were taken; that is, only through (1) continued investment of American capital abroad, and (2) a positive and prolonged effort to promote imports on a selective basis. These steps were never carried out.

Instead, a very different set of policies was adopted. The investment of capital abroad was not gradually curtailed; late in the decade it was abruptly shut off. Imports were never promoted; they were continuously excluded. The ultimate adjustment to the creditor position of the country (if any ultimate adjustment can be said to have taken place) was therefore effected under disastrous conditions. Critics could state the thesis in much harsher terms. The combination of a high tariff wall with relentless pushing of exports, they could say, was a tragic error, which had to be paid for. The payment was made by American investors who put their money into foreign bonds—and never got it back; by taxpayers who lost all hope of repayment of foreign governmental debts; and by farmers whose overseas markets were destroyed. Far from reading an appropriate lesson from its experience in the 1920's, the United States plunged forward to a worse error in the Smoot-Hawley Act of 1930.

Political and economic nationalism were matched by social nationalism in the field of immigration legislation. This was much more defensible, for from almost every standpoint impressive arguments could be cited for a sharp reduction in the influx of aliens. Culturally, a long interval was needed to complete the assimilation of the heavy immigrant population which had been accepted during the previous generation. Labor in America, as in Australasia, had become apprehensive that continued immigration would prevent a proper unionization of unskilled and semi-skilled groups, and so cripple the movement for wage increases. Problems of illiteracy, machine politics, second-generation criminality, and slum eradication were all complicated by the immigrant stream. It was widely believed that ignorant aliens of low living standards offered ready material for the anarchist and Communist agitator. Altogether, it was not strange that Congress in 1917 passed a literacy-test bill over President Wilson's veto.

The first restrictive bill, passed in 1921 and operative until 1924, limited the immigration of any national stock to 3 per cent of its total in the United States in 1910. A new law became necessary in 1924. Majority feeling was strongly in favor of maintaining the predominance of the northern and western European elements in the national texture. The impoverished and ill-educated southeastern nations of Europe had been contributing most of the immigration. A bill was therefore passed which made as the basis of apportionment the figures for the year 1890 instead of 1910, and reduced the inflow to 2 per cent of the total of any stock present in the country in that year. The law also provided for its own supersedence in 1927 by a more complicated "national origins" plan. The total number of immigrants admissible yearly was then to be fixed at 150,000, and national quotas were to be computed on the proportion of the number of American descendants of each nationality in 1920 to the whole population of that year. While application of this scheme offered many difficulties, in practice it meant that all immigration was reduced to a trickle. The annual quota allotted to the United Kingdom was 65,721—and few Britons now cared to emigrate; the annual quota allotted to Italy was but 5,802, and that to Poland but 6,524. Hungary, Greece, and Czechoslovakia all received quotas of less than 1,000.

A stinging provision of the 1924 law, the Japanese exclusion clause, had most unhappy consequences because of the needless insult it offered to a proud nation. Under Theodore Roosevelt a *modus vivendi* governing Japanese immigration had been reached in the Root-Takahira Agreement. Never reduced to a single document, and never submitted to the Senate, this stop-gap arrangement excluded all long-term settlers from Japan, while admitting students, teachers, travelers, and sojourning businessmen. Though on the whole it worked well, the Pacific Coast remained apprehensive of Japanese infiltration. California and Washington therefore passed laws which forbade the

sale or lease of farm land to Japanese. Public sentiment in Japan, offended by this legislation, was
further irritated by the failure of Americans at the
Peace Conference of 1919 (despite Wilson's sympathy with the idea) to help write the principle of
racial equality into the League Covenant. Tokyo
was again incensed when in the fall of 1922 the
Supreme Court decided, in *Ozawa* vs. *the United
States*, that Japanese were ineligible for citizenship.
Then in 1924 the immigration bill, under Far
Western pressure, substituted a rigid law for the
gentlemen's agreement by excluding from the country all "aliens ineligible for citizenship."

This was a flagrant affront, and its implications
of racial inferiority sorely wounded the island
people. Since the quota system would have limited
immigrants to 146 a year, the exclusion was quite
unnecessary. Secretary Hughes, who saw that it
would undo much of the good work of the State
Department on Far Eastern questions, attempted
to get the phraseology altered. He might have succeeded had not Ambassador Hanihara made a
thoughtless statement that the Act would have
"grave consequences." Instantly Congress, mis-
interpreting this as a threat, put its back up. Lodge
in a vitriolic speech accused Tokyo of attempted
intimidation, and the bill passed both houses. The
effect in Japan was instant. American goods were
boycotted, demonstrations were held in the great

cities, and a student who committed hara-kiri was lauded to the skies. Many Japanese who had previously been indifferent or friendly became filled with hatred of the United States.

Not a little ill-feeling was likewise generated in Europe by the 1924 Act. The Italian Government in particular expressed resentment, and Mussolini soon cited the closing of the old-time havens for emigrants as a justification for his expansionism. All eastern and southern Europe felt aggrieved. Numerous families were divided, children being separated from parents, and brother from sister. Slavic and Latin immigrants in large American cities labored under a sense of discrimination. Nor did the law by any means do all that had been expected of it in strengthening American homogeneity. Great numbers of Mexicans, French Canadians, and Puerto Ricans, all outside the quota, swarmed into the country, while a large body of illegal immigrants swelled their ranks. Yet the new policy was too strongly approved by the nation to be shaken.

Meanwhile, the question of the war debts opened an almost impassable gulf between American and Allied policy. A makeshift bridge was thrown across this chasm, but its rickety pillars collapsed within a decade. The Allies, whose losses in manpower as well as treasure had been staggering, naturally felt that in the achievement of a common victory lives might well be balanced against dollars. Americans, regarding the war as primarily a European conflict into which they had been unfairly dragged, felt that after rescuing France, Britain, Italy, and Belgium, they were being cheated by those whom they had saved. When the peace gave Britain, France, and Italy marked accessions of territory (though as mandates, not outright annexations), and provided for heavy reparations payments, Americans felt certain that every dollar lent by them ought to be repaid.

The network of intergovernmental obligations was exceedingly complex. The United States had made loans to, or otherwise accumulated a credit balance against, sixteen countries. Great Britain, whose advances to her Allies far exceeded her receipts from the United States, emerged from the war with payments due her from seventeen nations. France, debtor to the United States for a huge sum, was creditor to ten European nations. In the first year of peace, numerous Allied leaders urged that this whole fabric be swept aside by an all-round cancellation of debts, so that the single important financial question remaining would be German reparations. This, they argued, would give European currencies a solid basis, liberate trade by furnishing all the countries greater purchasing power, eliminate bickerings, and help great populations to get back to work. But to most Americans such pleas seemed a wily attempt by the debtors to escape their just obligations.

It was not as plain to Americans as it should have been that a distinction was evident between the British and the Franco-Italian attitudes. The British were ready to cancel debts owed them by other European nations in a sum equal to or greater than the whole debt owed to the United States. On paper, Great Britain was entitled to about twice as much from her Allies, including Russia, as she was supposed to pay America. London would have liked to cancel if America did so; it could not cancel unilaterally. The French and Italians, however, were never convinced that the debt to America had any moral validity whatever. This view was irritating to Americans, particularly as they found France under Poincaré inexorably harsh in her demands upon Germany and as both France and Italy were spending large sums on armaments. Congressmen, recalling that Wilson had asked for nothing in territory or reparations at Paris, refused to consider any readjustment of the principal.

From the beginning the British recognized the justice of debt payment and made it clear that they would try to discharge their obligations. While insisting that debts and reparations were indissolubly connected, they made early initial remittances. In 1923, when the Ruhr occupation proved that London and Paris could not work hand in hand, the British Government decided to fund its debt as the United States had suggested. Stanley Baldwin, Chancellor of the Exchequer, visited Washington, and on June 19 signed a debt agreement. The terms seemed to Englishmen very harsh. The loans had aggregated, with accrued interest, $4,600,000,000, practically all of which represented wartime payments or credits. The whole principal was to be returnable over sixty-two years, with interest at 3 per cent for the first decade, and 3.5 for the remaining period. To Americans, whose war bonds had borne an interest of about 4.25 per cent, the charge seemed low; to Britons, who remembered that in peacetime they had been able to raise money at between 2 and 3 per cent, it seemed exorbitantly high.

Parliament assented to the Baldwin-Mellon agreement only after a bitter debate. It acquiesced because Britain's prestige as financial leader of the world and her reputation for integrity seemed at stake; and also because many believed that long before the sixty-two years expired, America would be forced by events to revise the compact. The Senate, too, showed some reluctance in ratifying, many regarding the terms as excessively soft. General American sentiment, however, applauded the agreement.

Britain having led the way, France, Italy, and

other nations had to follow. The French debt, with accrued interest, was fixed at $4,025,000,000. No interest at all was to be paid for the first five years, and only 1 per cent for the next ten, while the average interest rate for the whole period was to be 1.64 per cent, or a little less than half the British rate. Italy, whose debt was funded at $2,042,-000,000, was let off with an average interest rate for the sixty-two years of only two-fifths of 1 per cent. In dealing with Belgium, the American Government drew a clear line between pre-armistice and post-armistice borrowings. On the former, amounting to about $172,000,000, no interest whatever was charged; on the latter, which came to $246,000,000, the interest averaged 1.79 per cent.

In negotiating these agreements, the World War Debt Commission, created by act of February 9, 1922, was instructed to arrange "just" settlements. This it interpreted as meaning that the entire principal must be repaid, although the interest might be adjusted; that payment should be made in moderate installments, extending over two generations; and that interest should be charged according to "capacity to pay." Obviously, the Commission arrived at a very rough kind of justice.

Throughout the negotiations the United States clung to the principle established by President Wilson, that Allied debts and German reparations

were distinct matters. This rule was reiterated by
Harding, Coolidge ("They hired the money, didn't
they?"), and Hoover. It became an *idée fixe*. Yet
to the common-sense view it was clear that a connection did exist, for "capacity to pay" depended
upon income from Germany. France, having lost
the greater part of her Russian, Turkish, and Bal-
kan investments, was unable to make payments to
the United States and Great Britain unless she received large sums from the Reich. Secretary Mellon in 1927 acknowledged the connection; for he
declared, in a letter to President Hibben of Prince-
ton, that except for Great Britain, the debt settlements did not require European nations to assume
a large burden of taxation, "since the sums paid us
will not come from taxation, but will be more than
met by the payments to be exacted from Germany."
When reparations ended, as a matter of fact, debt
payments were also close to their end.

The whole sum which the United States was
scheduled to receive under the various agreements
in force on July 1, 1931, came to more than twenty
billion dollars. So far as national policy went, this
sum was to be paid whether the world was prosperous or depressed, whether armaments were increased or reduced, and whether Germany furnished reparations or not. It was to be paid over a
tariff wall which was quite prohibitive. The British
soon pointed out that their debt, because of the

fall in prices, represented about twice as much in goods as they had received.

Though the United States did little in its handling of the war debts to promote concord, it lent expert assistance in two successive revisions of German reparations. From the beginning, these reparations had constituted an ugly problem. The peace treaty had set up a commission which was to be composed of permanent delegates from Great Britain, the United States, France, and Italy, with Japan and Belgium alternating as additional members. When the Senate failed to ratify the treaty, the commission lost its only impartial nation. The Germans thought the French rapacious in their demands; the French thought the Germans stubbornly obstructive. Before long, the problem had filled the German people with bitterness, produced sharp clashes among the former Allies, gravely disturbed international finance, and impeded world recovery. Altogether, the mishandling of reparations was unquestionably one of the roots of the Second World War. It was to Secretary Hughes's credit that he tried to promote an orderly settlement.

Briefly summarized, the American contribution lay in lending Europe two groups of experts, the first under Charles G. Dawes and the second under Owen D. Young, who in 1924 and 1929 mediated among bickering nations, helped furnish an expert study, and placed the reparations scheme on a more practical basis. In essence, they did something to modify the Versailles Treaty.

The first intervention, resulting in the so-called Dawes Plan, was an outgrowth of the French occupation of the Ruhr. Germany in 1922 failed to hand over her required deliveries of coal and timber; and though the default was involuntary, Premier Poincaré was determined to seize guarantees. On January 11, 1923, French and Belgian troops entered the Ruhr. Dominant British sentiment condemned this occupation, as well as the ensuing French attempt to set up a "revolver republic" in the Rhineland. The German people met the invaders with a passive resistance of heroic intensity. Just before the crisis developed, Hughes had delivered a speech at New Haven (December 29, 1922) in which he described the unhappy results of the reparations quarrel, declared that the United States could not arbitrate, and suggested that an international body of financial experts take up the problem, ascertaining, first, what could and should be paid and, second, what was the best method of transferring payments. The proposal had met widespread applause. After attending a meeting of the American Bar Association in London in the summer of 1924, Hughes went on to Paris and Berlin, and labored to convert French and German leaders to his plan. Poincaré was meeting serious difficulties. In the end, he forced Germany to give up its resistance; but his tactics had almost estranged Britain, had chilled public opinion in other countries, had brought the Reich to the brink of ruin, and had resulted in a disturbing fall of the franc. Before long his ministry fell.

The Dawes Plan, laid before the world on April 9, 1924, and accepted by the nations concerned that summer, essentially scaled down the German obligations. While no definite total was set, the best American expert (Harold G. Moulton in *The Reparation Plan*) estimated it at thirty-two billion gold marks. The standard annual payment was to be two-and-a-half billion gold marks, starting the fifth year. Germany was given assurances against any further foreign invasion, and received an immediate foreign loan of 800 million gold marks. Half a dozen years later the Young Plan, reported by a committee of experts on June 7, 1929, dealt with the situation anew. It fixed a reparation total of slightly more than eight billion gold marks, a far smaller sum than had ever before been considered; it readjusted the annual payments, dividing them into an unconditional and a postponable part; and it established a machinery for transfers in the form of the Bank for International Settlements.

By a significant feature of the Dawes Plan, an Agent-General of Reparations was to be appointed

to see the new program executed and to advise the
Reich in managing its finances. The post went to
Seymour Parker Gilbert, of Morgan and Company,
who proved an inspired choice. It was the duty of
this brilliant young man to supervise the revenues
pledged for reparations, which included railway
bonds and industrial debentures; to keep a watch-
ful eye upon the new central bank or Reichsbank
set up as a depository for reparations funds, which
possessed monopolistic powers over the issuance of
paper money; to transfer the reparations; and to
give constructive thought to fiscal policy. So long
as the Dawes Plan was in force, until May 17, 1930,
Gilbert furnished the Reich invaluable help in shaping its course sagaciously. He insisted, against much
opposition, that it should face its problems realistically and balance its budget.

At the same time, Gilbert made plain to the
Allies his conviction that the indefinite continuance of foreign controls over the German economy
was impossible. "As time goes on . . .," he reported
in December, 1927, "it becomes always clearer that
neither the reparations problem, nor other problems depending upon it, will be finally solved until
Germany has been given a definite task to perform
on her own responsibility." The Dawes Plan had
never been regarded as final. It was merely a settlement designed to last until confidence had been
restored and sufficient knowledge gained to permit

comprehensive settlement of reparations and connected questions. The Young Plan, giving Germany the responsibility of transferring her annual
payments into foreign currencies, put an end to the
work of the Agent-General.

When the Young Plan was completed, the United
States and most other nations were highly optimis-
tic. They expected reparations and debt payments
to continue their easy flow. World trade seemed
fairly prosperous; industrial production was un-
precedentedly high; many American circles believed
that a new economics had been born and that in
an unexampled age of plenty all poverty would
soon die a natural death. Superficially, America
was secure in the greatest wealth and power she had
ever known. Yet already signs of trouble were appearing. From its inception the new prosperity had
been uneven and spotty, skipping the farmer, stock-
man, miner, and the textile manufacturer. The
United States was soon to need a larger foreign
market more than ever; yet with insouciant faith
in outworn economic devices, the country had
raised a tariff wall which was blocking international exchanges. The disastrous crash of the stock
market revealed to perceptive Americans the unstable character of their economy.

"In many respects the most important character-
istic of our international transactions, and one
which establishes definite relationships between

them, is the necessity for an approximate balance between payments made to foreigners and payments received from them." So stated the Commerce Department in 1943. How was this balance secured? We have already indicated how artificially this was done. The United States in 1929, its last full year of prosperity, sold abroad $5,241 millions of merchandise, and imported $4,400 millions, giving it a favorable balance of $841 millions. It received roughly $800 millions more from payments on the war debt and on investments abroad. This made total receipts of approximately $1,640 millions from foreign debtors and consumers. What balanced these payments? The sums spent by American tourists abroad in 1929 reached nearly $500 millions. About $200 millions was sent back to foreign countries by immigrants working in the United States. This left a huge additional sum to be covered. It was supplied by nearly $1,000 millions which the United States lent to foreign borrowers that year, no less than $602 millions of it in direct investments. As the flotation of foreign bond issues declined, direct investment rose, an index of the booming economic expansion of the time.

In short, the United States had not only reshaped the structure of reparations in the Dawes and Young Plans; it had financed reparations by prodigious exports of capital. American dollars had made a Grand Tour from Yankee pockets to foreign borrowers (largely Germans or Germany's customers), from these borrowers to the claimants of reparations, and from the claimant governments back to America in the form of war-debt payments. In 1927–28, Germany borrowed abroad about five times the amount she had to pay in reparations. Thus it was that the Dawes Plan worked so smoothly. In similar fashion, American lending enabled the United States to export far more than it imported. It was delightful while it lasted; but it was essentially irrational, and a time lay just ahead when the insecure world was to slip with a crash from the shoulders of the Atlas who was sustaining it.

CHAPTER IV

WILLIAM JENNINGS BRYAN, when the head of the State Department, had negotiated a series of treaties which he fondly hoped would mark a long step toward world peace. Borrowing from rules elaborated at the Hague Conference of 1907 for fact-finding commissions to deal with international disputes, he persuaded thirty-five nations to accept the principles of his "cooling off" plan. It provided that permanent international commissions should be set up between the United States and each signatory power to investigate and report upon any issue which threatened peace. One year was to be allowed for the investigation, and while it was being made, neither country could go to war; only when the report was issued might they do so.

These "cooling off" treaties had two main weaknesses. One was that if all nations created an overlapping series of bilateral international commissions, more than three thousand such bodies would be required to cover the globe. The other was

forcibly stated by Theodore Roosevelt in a blister-
ing commentary in the *Outlook:* it was the lack
of any apparatus for enforcement. "Nothing can
be truer," Lodge wrote to Roosevelt, "than your
main theme of the folly, if not wickedness, of making treaties which have no force and no intention
of enforcement behind them." Bryan's treaties soon
passed into the limbo of the forgotten. No disputes
were ever submitted under them, and by 1927 only
three were in full operation, those with Denmark,
Sweden, and Portugal. But the appropriate lesson
pointed out by Roosevelt was never drawn.

How could the world's militarists and aggressors be placed in fetters, and peace guaranteed?
The state of public sentiment made Washington's
answer to this riddle cautious. To promote world
peace while resolutely avoiding substantial commitments in its behalf; to encourage general amity
while rejecting the idea of any collective security
system; and to preach international concord while
pursuing paths of economic nationalism—these
were the policies of three American Administrations after 1921. The policies of other nations were
equally timid and halting. They led to an attempt
to establish world peace upon a system of gradual
disarmament, supplemented by denunciations of
war, and culminating in a paper scheme for "out-
lawing" it. The emphasis laid upon disarmament,
or rather arms limitation, harmonized with the

pacifist ideals of America, Great Britain, and France. It had a delusive glitter of logic, for if all countries possessed but a feeble capacity to wage wars, then surely wars would become fewer and smaller. But in the end the system proved futile and dangerous. Its effect was to weaken the nations which had a substantial stake in the preservation of peace, while leaving those with a possible stake in war free to rearm. The pacifist surge broke up the alliance which had won the First World War without substituting for it an efficient mechanism of collective security.

The problem of disarmament presented two main aspects; one, the reduction of land forces in Europe, the other the reduction of the principal navies— those of America, Britain, France, Japan, and Italy. The first task was primarily the responsibility of Europe and the League. The second was largely the responsibility of the United States, which emerged from the war with one of the world's two greatest navies, and a financial ability to increase its strength which no other power could approach. In both spheres the attainment of a certain degree of security had to precede disarmament, and this seemed easier to arrange among the naval powers than in regard to the land forces of Europe. The first great victory for disarmament was therefore scored under the aegis of the United States—but it was a victory of dubious quality.

The League powers and the one great power outside Geneva necessarily looked upon the question,
at the outset, from different points of view. The
principle governing the chief members of the
League was stated in 1920 by Lloyd George. A general limitation of armies and navies, he declared,
was imperative unless the Covenant was to become
a sham and mockery. Heavy armaments would be
proof that the promoters of the new world organization had no faith in its efficacy. In other
words, disarmament had to be geared to the
League's system of collective security. As the first
flush of European faith in a bright new world
order died away, the American distrust of collective
security and of sanctions began to permeate other
nations. The Canadian delegates to the First
League Assembly proposed voiding Article Ten (on
the territorial integrity of members), and suggested an agreement that no member-state should
be bound to engage in war unless with the consent
of its Parliament. It was soon tacitly accepted that
the correct interpretation of Article Ten was that
each member should decide for itself the extent to
which it was bound to support the Article by
armed strength. The Second Assembly, in 1921,
meanwhile adopted nineteen resolutions which
weakened Article Sixteen with respect to the use
of economic sanctions. The spirit of nationalism
was increasingly strong in Canada, Australia,

South Africa, and New Zealand as well as Great Britain; and many people in the British Commonwealth of Nations tended to think of the League as valuable chiefly for consultation and the focusing of world opinion, and to distrust its collective-security mechanisms on the ground that they were about as likely to breed wars as prevent them. Nevertheless, member-states did wish to use the League system in reducing armed forces.

The United States did not. Since its Government had rejected the League system, it could approach disarmament in more elementary terms. To achieve naval reduction, the basic requirement was simply a broad regional understanding in the Pacific. Anglo-American amity could be taken for granted. In the Far East, the reconciliation of China and Japan, the guarantee of the Open Door, and a naval adjustment which would make it highly risky for the Japanese forces and the combined Anglo-American forces to attack each other —these were the main desiderata for arms limitation. No hopes or fears regarding an elaborate collective machinery for peace were involved.

Much American opinion in 1921 remained bitterly unreconciled to the rejection of the League. The Harding Administration found it important to do something to placate the formidable army of Republicans as well as Democrats who felt that the

nation was betraying its duty to humanity. The
President had so frequently declared that international conference might somehow take the place of
the League that it seemed indispensable to put this
idea into practice. A number of motives, including the desire for economy, thus suggested to Republican leaders the calling of a world disarmament
conference. The foremost figure in the movement
was William E. Borah, who had come out of Idaho
to take a Senate seat in 1907. A rugged, forceful
man of thunderous voice, progressive doctrines,
and far greater reputation for negative than constructive activity, Borah had voted reluctantly for
our entry into the World War, had urged a conscription of wealth while opposing any conscription of men, and had taken a leading part after
the conflict in repealing repressive legislation. His
opposition to the League had been founded on
principle, and though the most implacable of the
Senate "irreconcilables," he retained Wilson's full
respect. He was a stout believer in peace. Immediately after the election of 1920 he had presented a resolution for a disarmament conference;
and while Harding and Hughes were at first chilly,
Borah's insistence, the pressure of public opinion,
and the fact that Great Britain would act if the
United States did not, forced the Administration
to acquiesce. On May 25 the Senate unanimously
passed Borah's amendment to the Naval Bill re-

questing the President to invite Great Britain and
Japan to a conference charged with the substantial annual reduction of naval programs during the
next five years.

A striking part in the general movement was
played by the issues which already threw a heavy
shadow over the Orient. The aggressive territorial
expansion of Japan was now arousing deep American apprehension. At the Paris Conference, Japan
had maintained her foothold in Shantung and,
though she had agreed informally to restore the
area to China in the near future, she hoped to keep
her economic primacy there. In the teeth of Aus-
tralian opposition, the Japanese had obtained a
League mandate over all the former German-owned
islands north of the equator. This brought the
Japanese flag down south and east of the Philippines, uncomfortably close to the northern shores
of Australia, and within striking distance of two
prized American islands, Guam and Midway.
Would Japan really keep her pledge to restore
Shantung? Those who doubted it pointed to the
steady penetration of Japanese interests into Manchuria and the notorious Twenty-One Demands on
China in 1915. As a result of these demands, the
Japanese control of the South Manchuria Railroad
had been extended to ninety-nine years, and Japanese subjects (including Koreans) had been given
the right to lease land in South Manchuria. Irre-

pressible Japanese leaders were talking of a protectorate over all China.

The spirit of John Hay and his "Open Door" for trade and cultural influences was still potent in America. For reasons political, commercial, and idealistic, the United States felt itself committed to maintain the sovereign right of the Chinese to govern themselves, even though the country was torn by misrule, local anarchy, and civil war. China in American eyes was still for the Chinese, and Japan should aid her, not victimize her. Ever since 1899 the stopping of Japanese expansion had been a dominant motive in American policy.

Still another issue concerned the Anglo-Japanese alliance, first concluded when in 1902 both countries feared the encroachments of Czarist Russia. It was purely defensive; and when it was renewed, the British added an annex declaring expressly that it could never be used against the United States. But it was increasingly disliked not only in the United States but in Canada and Australia, for it seemed to throw the moral weight of Britain behind certain aggressive Japanese policies which citizens of America and the Dominions detested. Canada protested so strongly on the subject that Great Britain had suggested a conference on Pacific problems to Washington even before Hughes could take action.

All these issues were complicated by the growing

movement toward a frantic naval competition. The Japanese-American tension had created powerful demands in both nations for more battleships, cruisers, and bases. The American naval program of 1916, which included ten new battleships and one battle cruiser, was pushed with an energy which could not but alarm Tokyo. If the United States persisted in heavily outbuilding Japan, it would within a few years also be far superior to Britain in every department save light cruisers. The British would inevitably strive to keep up, and the costly competition would then extend to France and Italy.

When on August 11, 1921, the Harding Administration invited Britain, France, Italy, and Japan to meet in Washington just three months later, other Pacific powers were included. To deal with the Far Eastern problem, Belgium, the Netherlands, Portugal, and China were asked to send delegates. The various nations came with different hopes and intents. The French delegation anticipated a collision between the British and Americans, from which they could make capital. The British delegates, led by Arthur Balfour, whose tact and intellectual power made a strong impression, were anxious to obtain an accord with the United States, and they were assisted in this by the treaty establishing the Irish Free State, which was ratified by the Dail Eireann in January, 1922, and which gave great satisfaction throughout America. The Dutch were anxious to safeguard their rich and defenseless East Indian possessions. Naturally the Japanese displayed little enthusiasm for the Conference; yet their delegation under the liberal Hanihara proved highly conciliatory.

Of the four great goals of the Conference, one stood preeminent in importance. These four objectives were, first, to bring to an abrupt end the perilous naval competition already under way; second, to persuade Britain to give up the narrow Japanese alliance in exchange for a broad agreement of more constructive character; third, to induce Britain, the United States, France, and Japan to agree to respect each other's rights in the Pacific and to confer if any dispute broke out; and fourth, to unite all the Eastern powers in a pledge to respect Chinese sovereignty and the Open Door principle. It was this fourth object which gave the work of the Conference whatever enduring character it achieved. China was the rich quarry, the great unstable element, the half-helpless, half-formidable power in the East. The fascination which her potential wealth exercised upon the Japanese militarists was all too plain; their eyes glittered when they looked at her. If China were made free, strong, and a source of equal trading opportunities for all, then naval rivalries need give the Pacific powers little anxiety.

On November 12, the opening day, a remarkable body of delegates took their places in beautiful Memorial Hall in Washington. Secretary Hughes headed the American group, with Elihu Root, Henry Cabot Lodge, and Oscar Underwood behind him; Arthur Balfour was flanked by able men from the Dominions; France had sent Premier Aristide Briand, René Viviani, and the much-liked Jean Jules Jusserand; Wellington Koo and Alfred Sze represented China; and along with Hanihara, Baron Tomosaburo Kato, the Naval Minister, was ready to speak for Japan. The eyes of the world were fixed on the gathering. Some of the most famous of living writers, such as H. G. Wells, had come to report it. President Harding made a formal address of welcome; and then Hughes, as chairman, delived an address which gave the nations a delightful shock.

"The time has come, and this conference has been called," he said, "not for a general resolution or mutual advice, but for action." And action he offered in full measure! He proposed a ten-year stoppage of construction in capital warships. The United States should scrap all of the fifteen capital ships of the 1916 program on the ways (one battleship had been completed), with numerous other vessels, amounting in all to some 845,000 tons; Great Britain should stop the building of her four new *Hoods* and scrap other vessels; and Japan should make roughly proportionate sacrifices. Altogether, he suggested that the three chief naval powers should destroy sixty-six capital ships built or building, aggregating 1,878,000 tons. Though admirals were shocked, the plain people of all lands were delighted. "In thirty-five minutes," wrote a British correspondent, "Secretary Hughes sank more ships than all the captains of the world have sunk in a score of centuries!" The galleries of Memorial Hall rang with applause. Hughes also proposed that the existing ratios of naval strength should be accepted for the duration of the treaty. He knew that the Navy Department objected strongly to any sharp diminution of tonnage, and this maintenance-of-ratio plan was designed to placate high naval officers.

The Japanese disliked the inferior status into which they were thrust, and the French were even more deeply hurt; but in the end the powers accepted for the United States, Britain, Japan, France, and Italy the respective ratios of 5: 5: 3: 1.75: 1.75. In capital ships, the naval treaty provided for Hughes's ten-year holiday; but thereafter, unless the treaty were extended, new vessels (as distinguished from replacements) could be freely built. Aircraft-carrier tonnage was limited. All efforts to cut down the tonnage of smaller vessels, unfortunately, failed in the face of French intransigence. Anxious not to be reduced to hopeless subordination on the sea, France insisted upon at least 90,000 tons of submarines; her demands prevailed; and thereupon the British declined to accept any reduction in destroyers and in cruisers of less than 10,000 tons.

The Anglo-Japanese treaty was really dead when the Conference began, and had only to be buried. London could not think of extending it against the strong Canadian-American opposition. It was replaced by a vaguer and broader agreement, the text written by Secretary Hughes. Four naval powers, the United States, Britain, France, and Japan, pledged mutual respect for one another's rights in their possessions in the Far East, and agreed to submit to a joint conference any dispute which threatened difficulties. They also bound themselves to full consultation if their rights were ever threatened by the aggressions of another power. Conference upon any dispute, conference upon any outer threat—but beyond conference they would not agree to go! The fact that a promise to confer meant precisely nothing was as yet imperfectly grasped.

A virtual adjunct of this Four-Power Treaty was the engagement of the United States, Britain, and Japan, in the nineteenth article of the naval treaty, to maintain the existing status respecting fortifications and naval bases in the Pacific. Japan was thus bound, on paper, not to fortify the Kuriles,

Bonins, Formosa, or the islands obtained under mandate from Germany; Great Britain was not to augment the strength of Hong Kong or other holdings east of 110° east longitude (which left her free to develop Singapore) ; and, most significant of all, the United States was estopped from making Guam, the Aleutians, and the Philippines defensible. The outer bounds of American power in the Pacific were marked by Hawaii.

Since the Hamlet of the piece was China, it was the Nine-Power Treaty, signed on February 6, 1922, which stood as the most important fruit of the Conference. Could the chaotic, bandit-harried, floundering Chinese nation be so safeguarded that it might work out its own destinies? The Chinese pressed earnestly for abolition of the extraterritorial rights and special economic privileges granted to certain other powers, but gained only limited concessions. The Nine-Power Treaty (signed by Portugal, the Netherlands, Belgium, and Italy, as well as the greater powers) did, however, lay down some benevolent "principles and policies." So far as mere words could do anything, it provided for the sovereignty and territorial integrity of China and full freedom in trading with her. The signatories were to help China maintain an effective government, to use their influence in behalf of equal opportunity for commerce and industry, and to refrain from seeking exclusive rights.

Special agreements outside the Nine-Power Treaty provided for complete restoration of Chinese sovereignty in Shantung, which Japan now nominally evacuated; for full Japanese withdrawal from Siberia; for careful restudy of the issue of extraterritoriality; for confirming the Japanese mandate over Yap, but with recognition of American cable rights; and for determining several other small problems. On paper, the treaty was a document of scope and dignity. Unhappily, it merely *assumed* that all the nations would live up to their promises, and not a word in it provided for any enforcement of its provisions.

The fundamental weakness of the Nine-Power Treaty was that it beguiled the peace-loving powers into believing that they had really found a way to preserve justice, democracy, and equal trading rights in the Far East. An ironclad engagement to use collective force against any transgressor would have given the treaty validity, but neither Elihu Root, who wrote much of its text, nor the Administration, nor American sentiment, would risk any such commitment. Chinese integrity and independence were to be protected—so long as it cost nothing.

For a few years special circumstances assisted in cozening the peace-loving nations. The Japanese Foreign Office, guided by Baron Kijuru Shidehara, was for the time being almost a model of reason and equity. Its treatment of China was not only just but generous. Casting aside hostility to the Soviet Union (though not its dread of Communism), Tokyo recognized the Russian Government in 1925, and withdrew from northern Sakhalin. A tight rein was fixed upon the miltarists, the army was reduced, and encouraging latitude was given in democratic ideas. At League meetings the delegates could almost always count upon a display of good will by the Japanese representatives. Great Britain, in particular, continued to feel that Japan was a powerful buttress of peace in the Orient.

Behind this liberal Japanese policy lay a complex of factors, ranging from the chastening effect of the great earthquake of 1923 to the conviction of many educated Japanese that the nation's political maturity made a democratic type of government logical. But would Tokyo long continue on the course charted by Shidehara? The answer proved to be "No." When Japan altered her course, the Nine-Power Treaty constituted no impediment to her aggressions.

In short, a profound miscalculation lay beneath the Nine-Power Treaty. It was the belief that mere conferences, invocations of good will, and written pledges could save the United States from the troublesome necessity of joining a collective security system. The League offered a system of world-wide scope; any enforcement clauses written

into the Nine-Power Treaty would have set up a
system of limited scope. A lesser miscalculation lay
in America's easy belief that the Japan of Shidehara, friendly to Western trade and to a good-
neighbor policy, would endure indefinitely; that
the aggressive Japan of the Twenty-one Demands
would not reappear.

Since the Nine-Power Treaty was the essential
underpinning of the naval-limitation treaty, its
collapse would (and in time did) bring down the
naval reduction scheme in ruins. But the scheme
itself involved a miscalculation. It was supposed
that the reduction of capital (that is, long-cruising)
ships to limited numbers in a 5:5:3 ratio would
make it impossible for Britain or the United States
to attack Japan, and for Japan to attack Britain
or America. A fair balance would thus be established. But as a matter of fact the limitation favored the Japanese. Had competition remained
open, they could never have afforded the money to
build against the United States and Great Britain.
Unrestricted building of short-range vessels gave
Japan an immense advantage in the seas washing
Manchuria, China, the Philippines, and the Dutch
Indies. Moreover, while the Japanese needed to
think of but one naval sphere, the British had to
think of the North Atlantic, Mediterranean, Indian
Ocean, and Malaysian waters; the United States
had to think of the North and South Atlantic,

Caribbean, and Gulf. Accordingly, Britain and America were dangerously weakened for their wide responsibilities, while Japan was temporarily unchallengeable in her narrow waters. But for the time being, in 1922, the world hailed the Washington Conference as a momentous object lesson in the advancement of peace by mutual compromise.

Nothing better illustrated the unwillingness of isolationists to take even very slight risks of international involvement than the fate of the World Court in the Senate. With the creation of this Court, the Republican party was historically identified. Its basic concept had been advocated by the American delegation which Theodore Roosevelt sent in 1907 to the Second Hague Conference. When a commission of jurists drew up the Court statute in 1920, no man contributed more to it than Elihu Root. In 1921 the League Assembly and Council elected eleven judges, one of whom was John Bassett Moore. President Harding had promised in his inaugural address that the United States "would gladly join" a world court, and his Cabinet earnestly supported the organization. The President was in no haste to move. But feeling certain that public opinion was "overwhelmingly in favor of our full participation," Harding finally summoned courage to urge the Senate (February 24, 1923) to act. A great majority of newspapers, civic organizations, and public leaders gave him support. To reassure the doubtful, Hughes himself had framed four reservations: the United States should not enter into any legal relation with the League or obligation under the Covenant; it should participate in all proceedings for the election of judges; it should pay such share of the Court's expense as Congress might determine; and the statute of the Court should not be changed without American consent. Administration spokesmen took the line that the Court had no real connection with the League, and that it constituted an essential advance toward an ordered peace.

But the isolationists were in strategic position to stifle the demand for adherence. Still controlling the Senate Committee on Foreign Relations, they held up the proposal, taking no action while Lodge and Borah explained that they were for *some* court, but against this one. When President Coolidge, who succeeded Harding in the summer of 1923, renewed the Court proposal in December, his plea went unheeded. A Democrat, Senator Swanson of Virginia, finally introduced a resolution for accepting Court membership on the Harding–Hughes terms. Thereupon a new peril was bruited to the country—the alleged danger that the World Court might give an advisory opinion to the League on some matter touching American interests, such as the Monroe Doctrine or the international debts. While the opinion would be in no sense binding, it might embarrass the republic. As a matter of fact, the Court never showed any disposition to hand down embarrassing advisory opinions, and in 1923 flatly refused to furnish one in the Eastern Carelia case because it would have offended Russia.

After months of delay had slipped into years, a drastic fifth reservation was added to the American stipulation. This provided that the Court should not, without American consent, "entertain any request for an advisory opinion touching any dispute or question in which the United States has or claims an interest." In January, 1926, the Senate finally voted adherence under this and the older conditions, 76 to 17. Friends of the Court pointed out that the phrase "claims an interest" really gave the United States an unlimited power to block action on advisory opinions, for America could *claim* anything.

The question at once arose whether the forty-eight nations which were now members of the Court would agree. Obviously no one could expect so many governments to return meek assents separately, and the Senate majority took the position that even one refusal would keep the United States out of the Court! When the League Council closed its sitting in March, 1926, Austen Chamberlain proposed that a conference of member-nations should be held late in the summer to discuss the American proposals. Twenty-two countries duly sent representatives, who cordially agreed that the United States should be guaranteed a position of equality. They suggested, however, that the manner in which it should give the consent provided for in the fifth reservation should be subject to a future understanding between the American Government and the Council.

Up to this moment, the obstruction offered the Court membership had centered in the Senate. Coolidge had ostensibly been a warm friend of American adherence. But isolationist feeling had apparently been growing. The dozen militant irreconcilables in the Senate, headed by Borah, were more sternly intransigent than ever. The President had to make a speech in the Middle West, popularly supposed to be the center of isolationism, and before the American Legion, a strongly nationalist body. In this speech, on Armistice Day in 1926, he startled the country by indicating that he would uncompromisingly reject the suggestion that the United States should explain exactly the procedure it desired. "Coolidge the Lion Hearted" was the New York *World's* caption on its scornful editorial. Thus died all immediate hope of membership.

The explanation for the nation's perverse rejection of so innocuous a commitment as membership in an admirably functioning court of international justice lies in a complex of factors. The passions aroused by the fight against the League still smoldered. Any institution connected with Geneva, Woodrow Wilson, and the idea of a mobilization of world-wide forces to prevent war remained an object of violent suspicion on the part of millions. It was still easy to arouse powerful bodies of German-Americans and Irish-Americans against any international endeavor. Numerous conservative Republicans, believing their party committed to abstention from Old World affairs, hardened their hearts and closed their minds. Another factor was the influence of American prosperity in making preservation of the *status quo* seem a sacred duty. No entanglements abroad, high tariffs at home, stern debt collection, generous loans and mortgages for other nations—it all constituted a working system, and thus far it had apparently paid. Why tinker with it?

The United States could lay flattering unction to its soul, moreover, in reflecting that its purse strings were generously loosed to aid the homeless and starving all over the world. Standing in glorious independence, could not America do more for the weak and distressed than if caught up in the endless controversies of older lands? By 1928, flushed with prosperity and satisfied with their apparent security, the American people seemed confirmed in their choice of isolationism. In the Presidential campaign of that year both candidates substantially ignored the League issue. Hoover, who in 1920 had thought it vital to the world that America subscribe to the Covenant, had long since turned his back on Geneva. Alfred E. Smith cautiously skirted the subject in public and repudiated the League in private. Once elected, Hoover spoke after a fashion that delighted bitter-enders. Collective security, he said on Armistice Day in 1929, was not for America.

Meanwhile, the summer of 1928 had witnessed the fruition of another remarkable effort to exorcise war by the incantation of unsupported treaties— the effort that gave birth to the Kellogg-Briand Pact or Pact of Paris. Back of this grand gesture lay a variety of regional movements for peace. The Washington Conference agreements had created part of the requisite atmosphere of confidence. The Geneva Protocol for the Pacific Settlement of International Disputes, introduced at the Fifth League Assembly in 1924 by Prime Ministers MacDonald and Herriot, had made its contribution. While it failed to gain sufficient adherence to become effective, the stigma it placed on aggressive war as an international crime was remembered. More directly useful were the Locarno agreements concluded in 1925 among the seven principal nations of western Europe. These embodied the principle of Article Sixteen of the Covenant that, if any nation pursued an aggressive course, then other nations should use force to compel respect for peace.

Most Americans heartily shared in that world-

wide applause of Locarno which, for a fleeting inter-
lude, made it seem a magic name in European
affairs, the open sesame to a more peaceful age.
Its chief architects were Gustav Stresemann, Aristide Briand, and Austen Chamberlain, Foreign
Ministers of Germany, France, and Britain. It was
Stresemann who, anxious to allay the old Franco-
German hatred, suggested a four-power guarantee
of the existing Rhine frontiers and a series of arbitration agreements among Germany and her
neighbors. He met with a ready response. Paris laid
down a number of stipulations, the chief of which
were that Germany should apply for entry into
the League, and that none of the new compacts
should interfere with France's obligations to her
Polish allies. These being accepted, the fall of 1925
found delegates of four major powers, Britain,
France, Germany, and Italy, and three lesser nations, Poland, Czechoslovakia, and Belgium, in conference. The discussion was carried on with an
absence of rancor and an optimism of outlook which
led men to speak of a new force—"the Locarno
spirit." Seven conventions to avert "the scourge
of war" by the "peaceful settlement of disputes of
every nature" were quickly initialed. One was a
treaty of mutual guarantees comprehending Great
Britain, France, Germany, Italy, and Belgium;
two were special treaties of guarantee between
France and Poland, and France and Czechoslo-

vakia; and four were arbitration treaties between Germany on the one side, and France, Belgium, Poland, and Czechoslovakia on the other.

By the great main compact, the four signatories stipulated that the western boundary of Germany fixed at Versailles should be maintained—which meant that Germany renounced all claim on Alsace, Lorraine, Eupen, Malmedy, and Luxembourg—and that the demilitarization of the Rhineland area should continue. Germany, France, and Belgium further agreed not to fight one another except in "legitimate defense," or in meeting a breach of the demilitarization scheme, or in fulfillment of League obligations. All the signatories pledged themselves to assist any nation which suffered from a violation of the treaty. Similarly, the treaties of France with Poland and Czechoslovakia stipulated that, if a breach of the Locarno agreements led to "an unprovoked recourse to arms," the three would lend each other immediate aid.

On the foundation laid by Locarno, by the Four-Power and Nine-Power treaties in Far Eastern affairs, by the growing concord of the American family of nations, and by Great Britain's concession of freedom to Southern Ireland and Egypt, the world seemed ready to erect a stately temple of peace. The League, with Germany's admission in 1926, became stronger than ever, while the World Court and International Labor Office were displaying a usefulness that commanded respect everywhere. To be sure, the Naval Conference of 1927 broke down. Convoked by President Coolidge in an effort to extend the 5:5:3 ratio to all naval categories, it met the opposition of France, which declined to send delegates on the ground that naval limitation could not be disengaged from the general problem of disarmament. The French wanted security guarantees which the United States would not give. Italy also held aloof; and when the American, British, and Japanese representatives met in Geneva in June, they fell into utter deadlock. This was primarily because the Americans wanted a small number of large cruisers, while the British desired a large number of small cruisers; partly because the old American doctrine of freedom of the seas conflicted with Britain's possible duties in war under the League Covenant. Some big-navy lobbyists from the United States, it was later discovered, had labored to encourage the deadlock. Big-navy proposals did receive a marked impetus from the failure of the Conference, and Congress shortly authorized the building of fifteen cruisers and one aircraft carrier.

The first World Economic Conference, meeting almost simultaneously in Geneva (May, 1927), with five able Americans among the 194 delegates who responded to the League's invitation, fortunately accomplished more. Declaring that the time had come to lower tariffs, the Conference urged governments to prepare plans for diminishing by stages the barriers that hampered trade, and recommended long-term commercial treaties holding an unconditional most-favored-nation clause.

But regional arrangements like Locarno and the Four-Power Treaty were not sufficient. A scheme for the general renunciation of war, taking definite shape at this moment, caught the imagination of those who, in the phrase of an American publicist, wanted "policies of international cooperation which will not bring entanglements." An American campaign for the "outlawry of war" had been originated by a Chicago attorney, S. O. Levinson, developed and expounded by his friend C. C. Morrison, editor of the *Christian Century*, and ultimately taken up by Senator Borah. Levinson not only coined the phrase "outlawry of war," but, aided by Morrison, John Dewey, and Raymond Robins, organized a growing movement. Borah introduced a Senate resolution on the outlawry of war on February 14, 1923, and reintroduced it December 6, 1926. Dr. James T. Shotwell of Columbia University had meanwhile undertaken a similar crusade; and visiting M. Briand on March 22, 1927, he suggested that the French accept the initiative by proposing a Franco-American treaty. On April 6, 1927, Foreign Minister Briand chose

the tenth anniversary of American entry into the
First World War to issue a statement which, after
declaring that France and America were morally in
full agreement, made a specific proposal: "If there
were need for those two great democracies to give
high testimony to their desire for peace and to furnish to other peoples an example more solemn still,
France would be willing to subscribe publicly with
the United States to any mutual engagement tend-
ing to outlaw war, to use an American expression,
between these two countries." The American idea
had become an international force.

For a fortnight Briand's modest proposal seemed
stillborn. This was not astonishing, for mere formal
assertions that war was unthinkable among France,
America, and Britain were too common to attract
attention. Then suddenly an influential voice sec-
onded the idea. Dr. Nicholas Murray Butler, in a
letter to the New York *Times* inspired by Dr.
Shotwell (April 25, 1927), pointed out that Briand
was speaking for the French Government, asked
whether the American people would respond favor-
ably, and argued that there could be no more fitting
tribute to those slain in the great war than this renunciation of war itself. Newspapers reprinted
salient passages of this letter. Forthwith a number
of men tried their pens upon a draft treaty, the
most important being that produced by Shotwell
and his colleague J. P. Chamberlain of Columbia

University. These drafts brought the outlawry of war into practical form for debate. It is significant that the language of the main clause written by Shotwell and Chamberlain, pledging the signatories never to attack each other or resort to war, was the language of Locarno; but whereas the Locarno agreement was backed by pledges of action, the American draft treaty had no provision for enforcement. Despite this weakness the scheme attracted wide attention abroad, receiving favorable comment even in Germany. Early in June, the French Government formally proposed to Washington that a treaty be drafted to abolish all possibility of war between the two nations.

By this time Frank B. Kellogg had been promoted (March, 1925) from the London Embassy to the Secretaryship of State. As a keen Government attorney who had prosecuted cases against the Union Pacific and the Standard Oil, a moderate Senator who had tried to arrange a compromise on the League, and a diplomat who had helped negotiate the Dawes Plan, he had accumulated ample experience. He was able and conscientious. At the same time, he had distinct weaknesses. Nearly seventy when appointed, his short frame bent, his hair snow white, his hands trembling, he was fussy, nervous, and oversensitive to public opinion. In dealing with Mexico and other Latin-American countries he evinced an unfortunate disposition to bow to investment groups which wanted a "strong" policy. In some areas of foreign affairs he was crassly ignorant. Happily, however, he was sometimes capable of sudden enthusiasm for an idealistic cause and of grim persistence in supporting it. Both he and Coolidge disliked Briand's original proposal, fearing that a Franco-American agreement might excite hostility in Europe as an apparent entente of the two nations. Indeed, no American of importance from the outset liked the French plan of a mere binational pact. Borah, in an eloquent speech at Cleveland, had hastened to assert that the treaty renouncing war should be multinational. Convinced of this fact, Kellogg in his reply to Briand on December 28, 1927, maintained that all nations should take shelter under the new roof. But he was fired with a real passion for the new concept. Talking with Coolidge, he laid eloquent arguments for an ambitious set of world treaties before the taciturn Vermonter, and finally committed the Administra-in two sentences:

Coolidge: "We can do that, can we not?"

Kellogg: "Yes, I think there is no question that we can make such a treaty with all the nations of the world and that it will be ratified."

From the moment of his December note to Briand, the Secretary was in charge of the plan, for the French, willing to embrace America but not the whole world, grew lukewarm. Kellogg's belief was that the treaty must be restricted to a brief statement renouncing war as an instrument of national policy; that it should initially be agreed to by a small group; and that other countries should then be invited to sign. He believed also in assiduous efforts to enlist world opinion. The negotiations must be conducted in the open. With peppery tenacity, he carried forward his policy. Old World diplomatists who had shared Austen Chamberlain's opinion that outlawry was "pure American bunk" and State Department men who talked of it as "the old man's folly" were forced to toe the line. The Secretary's enthusiasm became infectious. Cultivating the press, he had also the wisdom to insist that the treaty was bipartisan, a Democratic as well as Republican undertaking.

The climactic scenes as Kellogg arrived in Paris to sign his pact, August 27, 1928, were inspiring. A distinguished gathering, in which Briand, Stresemann, and Austen Chamberlain were conspicuous, met in the great hall of the Foreign Office; the Swiss Guard led a stately procession to the clock room for the signing; and Briand delivered a striking address. Delegates from fifteen nations appended their names. The American Senate ratified the following January, 85 to 1. By midsummer of 1932, sixty-two acceptances had been received.

The high hopes placed upon the pact were soon to seem curiously unreal. James T. Shotwell, writ-

ing on "Japan's Renunciation," envisaged a new
era of concord in the Pacific; Briand himself declared that the pact was "a direct blow against the
institution of war, a blow against its very life." It
contained a solemn pledge that the signatories
would renounce war as an instrument of national
policy and seek no solution of disputes except by
peaceful means. But where were the sanctions to
make this good? The answer of the authors was
that sanction lay in moral forces, in public opinion.
But did this really mean anything? A number of
nations made reservations in granting their adherence, interpreting the "outlawry" in such
fashion as to permit war in self-defense, in vindication of existing treaties, and in support of the
League Covenant. Obviously, the zone between defensive and offensive war might often become hazy.
Obviously, too, the moral force of *world* opinion
counted as yet for little. Nations had never hesi-
tated to set themselves, in great crises, against that
vague and alien entity and had frequently delighted
to defy it. A strong home opinion and strong collective sanctions were the only forces which could
really outlaw war.

The Pact of Paris was valid merely in so far as
it was supported by the League Covenant, Locarno,
and systems of defensive alliances. Beyond that it
proved worthless. It gave the peace-loving nations
a momentary access of moral enthusiasm; but it

also deluded some into believing that they held a new buckler of steel, when it was but painted paper. In the long view it perhaps did more harm than good.

Yet for the moment men's spirits rose; a bright star had lighted up the skies; and under its effulgence a new approach to the problem of disarmament seemed possible. As we have said, this problem offered two main aspects, one the reduction of land forces in Europe, the other the limitation of the five great navies. To deal with the former, the League had set up its Preparatory Commission on Disarmament. The protracted deliberations of this body made little progress. Proposals by Maxim Litvinov of Russia for complete and final disarmament by land, sea, and air, with similar demands by German leaders for general reductions, encountered opposition from the Western powers. The main reason, of course, was that such action would place nations of small population, like France, at the mercy of great neighbors, like Germany and Russia, which could rapidly arm their overwhelming manpower. In the naval field, the failure of the 1927 conference had left a bitter taste. When next year the Hearst press revealed a secret agreement between Britain and France, by which Paris had promised future support of the British stand on naval limitation while London engaged to withdraw its objections to the French position on trained military reserves, ill-feeling in America was heightened. But the Pact of Paris improved the tone of international intercourse and made a new approach possible.

President Hoover, taking office in March, 1929, was anxious to achieve naval reduction, for his Quaker ancestry and business training gave him a love of peace, he knew that a diplomatic stroke would lend éclat to his Administration, and he believed in reducing expenditures. Charles G. Dawes, veteran Middle Western businessman and former Director of the Budget, was sent as Ambassador to London to prepare the ground. He promptly declared that the failure of the 1927 conference was a failure of method, not individuals, and that both nations agreed that the mistake must be retrieved. Ramsay MacDonald began his second term as Prime Minister in June, 1929; he was a determined pacifist and a friend of the United States, and he met the American approaches cordially. As a gesture of good will he announced in July that he would suspend all work on two cruisers and slow down other naval construction. By September so much progress had been made that a personal consultation of MacDonald and Hoover seemed expedient.

The Prime Minister, arrived in Washington, was soon delivering a tactful address to the Senate and retiring with Hoover to the President's week-end

camp on the Rapidan River. Here, under golden
October leaves, the two chiefs of state sat on a
log and gave a whole morning to discussion of
Anglo-American relations. They were congenial
personalities. Both had begun life as very poor
boys, both had worked their way up by hard labor,
both were devoted to peace, and both had great
idealism and vision. Their practical discussion
cleared away so many obstacles that on October 7
invitations to the Naval Conference were released
to Japan, France, and Italy, with intelligence that
the British and American governments had reached
an agreement in principle on the vexatious question of big and small cruisers.

The Conference began in London in January,
1930. Out of three months of negotiation finally
emerged a compromise agreement, the Naval
Treaty of London, which was received in the three
principal countries involved, America, Britain, and
Japan, with a curious medley of applause and
criticism. Whether the decisions taken ultimately
benefited or injured the cause of peace is a debat-
able question. France and Italy, quarreling over
the question whether they were to have mathe-
matical parity (for France maintained that as she
had an Atlantic coast to defend this would mean
inferiority for her in the Mediterranean), declined
to sign the most important part of the compact.
Paris still wanted political guarantees which

Britain and America refused. But the other three powers reached an agreement which, whatever its ultimate disadvantages to the two greatest, forestalled any immediate competition in building huge new navies.

The basic foundation of the compromise lay in the fixing of an over-all tonnage ratio among the three powers, combined with an allocation of the total tonnage to different categories. This was subject to subsequent transfer of a proportion of the tonnage from one category to another on due notice. It was a complicated arrangement, but it offered a means of reconciling the differing demands of Tokyo, London, and Washington as to heavy cruisers, light cruisers, and destroyers. Of large cruisers of the eight-inch-gun type the United States was granted 180,000 tons, Great Britain 146,800, and Japan 108,400. Of the smaller six-inch-gun cruisers, Great Britain was given 192,000 tons, the United States 143,500 tons, and Japan 100,450 tons. As for destroyers, both Great Britain and the United States were allowed 150,000 tons, and Japan 105,500. It would have suited the Anglo-American representatives to abolish all submarines. But this was impossible while France and Japan insisted on them, and the problem was solved by allowing each of the three main signatories a maximum tonnage of 52,700. All three agreed to a further holiday of five years in the construction of capital ships. Inasmuch as France and Italy were not bound by the tonnage restrictions accepted by the others, an "escalator clause" was introduced which permitted an emergency increase in tonnage if any of the three signatories found that considerations of national security required it.

Taxpayers interested in economy were pleased that a costly naval rivalry had been avoided; for the recent action of the United States (February, 1929) in passing the bill to construct fifteen new heavy cruisers and a new aircraft carrier at an estimated cost of $274,000,000 had aroused much alarm. Believers in Anglo-American amity as one of the chief cornerstones of world concord were delighted that so much irritation had been swiftly removed. The fact that all the parties to the Conference accepted rules which strictly limited submarine warfare was gratifying. In every nation, however, voices were lifted declaring that its naval security had been endangered. Although the total cruiser-destroyer-submarine tonnage allotted to Japan was decidedly above the 5:5:3 ratio, it fell short of the 10:10:7 ratio that Tokyo had demanded, and a member of the Japanese Naval Staff committed suicide. In Great Britain the fact that the replacement quota of cruisers permitted during the five-year period was only 9,000 tons excited much adverse comment.

Many years later two grave charges were brought

against this London Treaty: that it had heavily reduced the tactical value of the Anglo-American navies as against Japan, leaving that nation with every advantage of position, and that it had stunted the development of techniques of naval construction. When Britain finally had to fight on three continents and to guard convoys in every sea, she bitterly rued the fact that at London the Admiralty had lowered its estimate of "absolute needs" from seventy cruisers to fifty. On the whole, however, we may accept Mr. Stimson's statement that the London Treaty was a success; that the failure was that of the leaders in Japan, Germany, and Italy "who so quickly turned away from the peaceful path on which the treaty was a milestone."

Certainly at the moment the gains of the Conference seemed far to outweigh its risks. The adoption of the Young Plan appeared to have settled in satisfactory fashion the thorny problem of reparations. One great token of reviving friendship between Germany and her neighbors, the evacuation of the Rhineland, was within sight, for that operation was finally completed in June, 1930. At long last, near the close of 1930, the Preparatory Commission agreed upon a draft disarmament convention, and thus made possible a full-dress conference under League auspices on the general problem. From that conference much was hoped.

In Europe and the Far East, Russian agents seemed
to have ceased from their machinations, and the
fall of Zinoviev (head of the propagandist agency
called the Comintern) and his crew of plotters
gave men hope that the Soviet Union would re-
strict itself to home affairs. Save for the quarrel
which had broken out between Bolivia and Paraguay in the border region called the Chaco, peace
reigned throughout Latin America, where the
vexatious dispute over the Tacna-Arica question
was ended by a treaty of 1929. With the Kellogg
Pact being signed by one nation after another,
the outlook for a war-free world appeared hopeful.

Isolation—combined with kindly, cautious, non-
committal cooperation in political but not economic
fields—seemed a working system. So did the re-
generated system of *laissez faire* in the domestic
sphere. That crisis and collapse lay just ahead in
both home and foreign affairs would never have
been believed by the Americans who on January
1, 1930, celebrated one of the most delusively op-
timistic of their New Year's Days. The victory for
the moment remained with the abstentionists. They
could still treat with disdain the reproachful words
which Woodrow Wilson, then within three months
of his grave, had spoken on Armistice day in 1923.
The memory of battles fought on a high level of
vision and achievement, he declared, would be

"forever marred and embittered for us by the shameful fact that when the victory was won we turned our backs upon our associates, and refused to bear any responsible part in the administration of peace."

CHAPTER V

No President in our history had entered office with such varied and honorable international experience as Herbert Hoover possessed when elected in 1928. He knew Australia and the Far East by firsthand experience; he had long resided in London; he had directed the wartime relief of Belgium and the post-war relief of all Europe. The country felt justified in holding high expectations of his future policy. After offering the State Department to Borah, who refused it, he appointed as its head a cultivated and high-minded man of singularly varied experience. Henry L. Stimson, of old New England lineage, educated at Yale and the Harvard Law School, and trained in Elihu Root's law firm, had been Secretary of War under Taft, a special representative of President Coolidge in Nicaragua, and Governor-General of the Philippines. Of cool temperament, aloof personality, and scholarly tastes, he was unfitted for the rough and tumble of politics, as his defeat for the governorship of New

York in 1910 had shown. But he had an aggressive temper, and he made an industrious, astute, and fearless administrator. He liked to think of himself as "an advocate and a fighter." More international-minded than Hoover himself, more elastic of intellect, and far more tactful, he was indeed one of the ablest Americans of his time. He selected for Under-Secretary a liberal attorney of incisive mind, Joseph P. Cotton; and when Cotton died early in 1931, and William R. Castle became Under-Secretary, Stimson found his chief support in James Grafton Rogers, who was made Assistant Secretary of State.

Both Hoover and Stimson took office with well-defined conceptions of the proper conduct of foreign affairs. They believed that American policy must in great degree be based upon the Kellogg Pact. Both men also believed that strenuous efforts must be made to utilize the favorable opportunities presented by the Pact and the new world temper. Hoover liked to plan his moves carefully; Stimson preferred to reach his objective with a rush. The Administration pursued its high purposes with ability and energy. Its consultation with other governments, its friendly cooperation with the League, its withdrawal of marines from Santo Domingo, Haiti, and Nicaragua, and its attempt to persuade all peace-loving nations to deny the permanence of any situation infringing their treaty rights, constituted important forward steps. As the economic calamity of the Great Depression fell upon the world, however, some shortsighted acts of the Administration fatally clashed with its better policies.

Hoover had hardly settled himself in office when the skies of the globe darkened, misery began to engulf vast populations, fears for the future seized every nation, and an emergency arose second in gravity only to a great war. Within two years, nineteen countries were visited by revolutions or acute social disorders. The turn for the worse would largely have paralyzed abler statesmen than Hoover or Stimson. Nor was the President as keensighted as he should have been. The terrible stock market crash which stunned New York and American financial circles generally in the fall of 1929 was not at first regarded as the harbinger of a prolonged economic storm. While it ruined hundreds of thousands, and while many remembered the grim sequels of the similar crashes in 1873 and 1893, no widespread apprehension was initially felt in Europe or America. President Hoover made a series of reassuring statements, and Secretary of the Treasury Mills, various economists, and leading newspapers joined in the chorus. The stock market collapse, they said, left untouched our immense industrial potential and the reserves of wealth; it was essentially a mere investment panic.

The country seemed to have good reason for regarding the future with confidence. One index of world confidence in the United States—tragic enough in retrospect—was that of the $8,500,000,-000 of New York brokers' loans outstanding in September, 1929, more than three billions represented foreign money. Why, men asked, should the mere pricking of an artificial boom in the stock market of one nation bring the globe to its knees again?

But events quickly proved that grave weaknesses existed in the economic structure of the American nation and the world. The United States suffered from declining world markets, agricultural overproduction, and technological unemployment. Europe suffered from increasing political uneasiness, from the superior competitive power of many American and Japanese industries, from the strangulations of high tariffs and other trade restrictions, and from high armament costs. By the autumn of 1930, factory production and mineral output in the United States had heavily declined; industrial payrolls had dropped during the first ten months of the year by more than one-ninth; and freight-car loadings had fallen off in that period by more than one-eighth. Every businessman knew that the profits of enterprise were disappearing. The transfer of capital to Europe in the form of loans almost entirely ceased. As export and import trade, the globe over, declined month after month, Europe and America became conscious that an unhappier era had opened.

How would the depression affect the foreign policies of the United States? Would a feeling that all nations were economically interdependent lead it to new forms of cooperative world action? Or would the United States and other countries be chilled and frightened into policies of economic isolation? The answer was not long in doubt. President Hoover, who at first treated the panic as a purely national and transient phenomenon, adopted by the autumn of 1930 a radically different view. He told the American Bankers Association on October 2 that the depression was world-wide, its causes and effects lying only partly in the United States. Among the causes he pointed particularly to overproduction of raw materials, including rubber, copper, wheat, sugar, and silver. These gluts, he argued, had brought about a sharp fall of commodity prices, a reduction in the buying power of various nations, political unrest, and a lessened demand for the manufactured goods of Europe and the United States. In his message to Congress in December he repeated this analysis, declaring that the major forces of the depression now lay "outside the United States."

What, then, should the United States do? Did an international collapse of raw material prices, followed by a slump in the demand for manufactures, call for international remedies? Hoover held that it did not. In 1922, he argued, another world-wide depression had existed, and the United States had led the way out by efficient home measures for recovery. America had been able to perform this feat because of its remarkable degree of self-containment. Once more it should depend upon its own strength, and in doing so, should again assist other fallen peoples to rise. Congress, the major manufacturing interests, and much of the general public readily accepted Mr. Hoover's analysis. In fact, Congress anticipated the President, pushing the self-containment doctrine to a selfish extreme.

Never was the erratic quality of American foreign policy better illustrated than by that ill-timed explosion of economic nationalism, the Smoot-Hawley Tariff of 1930. American tariff-making had traditionally been an irrational process. Periodically, as new legislation was attempted, pressure groups representing strong manufacturing interests had taken control, and through legislative maneuvering and logrolling had passed acts which promoted a combination of local greeds and needs, but defeated the general welfare. So consistent was this pattern that any President invited disaster when he consented to tariff revision; the victorious special interests did not thank him for the result, while the country as a whole blamed him for it. Hoover's pledge in 1928 to assist agriculture had been interpreted as requiring a revision of duties on farm products. Under pressure from numerous groups, he called Congress (April 10, 1929) into special session to make "limited changes" in the schedules. Most Americans hoped for a scaling-down of duties, but once more logrolling industrial interests took control.

The result was the highest tariff in American history. Before the Hawley bill passed the House, lobbying, committee-room maneuvering, and bartering shoved up one set of duties after another. Farm products, which for the most part had an export surplus, and hence profited nothing, were given higher rates. So were other raw materials, including minerals; and then compensatory duties were placed on manufactured goods made from them. Textiles, dyestuffs, and chemicals were given special attention. Earthenware and glassware rates were boosted. When the bill went to the Senate, that body proposed an export bounty on all exports of farm products, and also suggested that the authority to reduce rates under the so-callled flexibility provision be vested not in the President (Coolidge having made this power a nullity) but in Congress. Hoover opposed both amendments. Finally, a conference measure following the main lines of the House bill was passed in June, 1930, nine months after the Wall Street panic.

Popular anger in the United States was even more vehemently expressed than after the frolics of rate-grabbing which gave the nation the McKinley Tariff of 1890 and the Payne-Aldrich Tariff of 1909. Hope that Hoover would veto the measure ran strong to the last. A thousand economists petitioned him to do so. But he lacked the foresight and courage, and with a public statement that "platform promises must not be empty gestures" he affixed his signature. All the dark predictions of the economists were duly realized. In fact, within eighteen months twenty-five nations had either revised their tariffs upward or were threatening such action, citing as justification the course of the United States.

The Smoot-Hawley Tariff, indeed, marked a great turning point in the history of the time. It was a significant event in that realm of international policy which finds economic action closely geared with political action. Time had been when an American tariff caused only transient irritation abroad. Foreign protests against the Payne-Aldrich Act in 1909 had shown that this era had ended, and that American tariffs had become major international events. Now the new law sent a wave of dismay around the world. America had abruptly stopped her export of capital; Wall Street's point-counterpoint of wild boom and wilder bankruptcy had given the whole globe a shock; and now the

United States seemed to be proclaiming war on international trade. Some nations had to export or die. Britain was one and Japan another, while Germany, France, Italy, Czechoslovakia all desperately needed trade outlets. The stock market crash and ensuing depression had represented a turn down the black road; now the Smoot-Hawley Tariff accelerated that turn. Hoover clung to his position to the end, declaring in 1932 that he was against the lower tariff advocated by Democrats, for "it would place Americans in competition with peasant and sweated labor products." Neither Secretary Stimson nor his able Economic Adviser, Herbert Feis, could have agreed, but the subject was outside their sphere.

A storm was raging; collective action to lessen it seemed more than ever impossible after America's step; and every nation ran blindly for shelter. Great Britain abandoned her historic policy of free trade, alleging sheer necessity. Under her tariff legislation of 1931–32, duties of 10 per cent were laid on most imports, with some commodities more steeply protected. Empire preference was a feature of this tariff, and the Ottawa Imperial Conference of 1932 resulted in a marked extension of the imperial preference system. At this gathering nine members of the Empire-Commonwealth were represented, and twelve trade agreements emerged. Britain not only pledged herself to import a wide range of Dominion goods for at least five years, but raised her duties on various foreign commodities in order to make preference effective. The Ottawa Agreements struck the United States a material blow, particularly in the British and Canadian markets. It was a significant fact that the originator and chairman of the Conference, Prime Minister Bennett of Canada, had been swept into office in 1930 partly on the wave of Canadian resentment against the Smoot-Hawley Act.

On the Continent of Europe an effort was made to induce the principal nations to turn to joint economic action. Various leaders proposed that the highly industrialized western countries pool their interests with the agricultural nations of eastern and southeastern Europe, the west giving preference to the farm products of the east, which in return would grant low rates on manufactured goods. The plan proved abortive, however, for no great industrial nation was able to look beyond its own borders. France, Italy, and Germany, striving to aid their own farmers, pushed yet higher the tariff on home-grown products. So steep was the French increase that by the middle of 1931 a bushel of wheat which cost 76 cents in Britain cost $2 in Paris.

Moreover, all the principal nations reinforced their tariff walls by quota restrictions limiting the amount of goods purchasable from abroad or requiring the admixture of a certain amount of home production with imported ingredients. Quota regulations soon became an impenetrable thicket. France, in time, placed 1,100 commodities on her quota lists, while even Britain fixed quotas for various foodstuffs. Inevitably, quota wars became entangled with tariff wars, and quota agreements were interlaced with preferential tariff compacts. If John Bull would buy so much butter and bacon from the Dane at agreed prices, then the Dane would buy so much coal from John Bull. By the middle thirties barter among nations reached a development which threatened to choke world trade to death. Meanwhile, the systematic debasement of currencies to stimulate exports played a part in the situation. Early in Hoover's last Congress, six bills were introduced in the House to protect American industry from what one measure termed "the effects of competition based on foreign currencies." Yet the United States was soon to play its full part in currency depreciation. With every new tariff, quota restriction, and bit of currency manipulation, international antipathies were intensified. Above the melee, war cries began to be heard—the loudest from Nazi throats.

In the United States, the movement for quotas prompted a demand for embargoes on oil, grain, butter, and Russian ores—it being alleged, for example, that the Soviet Union was dumping manganese ore. Economic nationalism found vent, also, in proposals for a *complete* stoppage of immigration. The House passed early in 1931 a bill which for two years would have limited immigration to 10 per cent of the existing quotas, but which the Senate dropped.

Even while Americans were trying to insulate themselves economically, events were demonstrating the impossibility of disentangling the nation from the common woe and weal. A wave of political unrest rolled around the planet. Drastic deflation in the raw materials produced by Latin America, followed by bankruptcy, debt defaults, general poverty, and unemployment, led to a series of revolutions. In eleven nations to the southward violent changes of government were effected in 1930–31. In still others, peaceful overturns took place, while in Cuba an armed revolt was suppressed by President Machado through a combination of military action and political and economic reforms.

The Latin-American revolts were remarkable for the force of popular feeling behind them, for the prominent role played by intellectuals, for their close relationship to unemployment and financial distress, and for their general success. They brought to power some strong new men to cope with the troublous time, such as Getulio Vargas in Brazil and José Uriburu in Argentina. In facing these revolutions, Washington displayed strict impartiality and disinterestedness. Hoover returned to the early American policy of recognizing *de facto* regimes, while he expressly disclaimed any idea of dollar diplomacy. But the revolts settled nothing important, or at least left the deep-seated maladies of Latin America untouched.

It was in Germany and Austria that the mingled currents of economic distress and political unrest produced results which most directly touched American interests. Central Europe was still an essential part of the world's industrial and commercial structure. The war had left it the most rickety and fragile part and, when it threatened to collapse, other nations seemed likely to be caught in the crash. The fall of the greatest Austrian bank, the Kredit-Anstalt, on May 11, 1931, made Europe quiver and alarmed all Americans who knew anything about international finance. It is a story worth telling in detail.

Austria, a nation of only seven millions, had achieved but a slow and partial recovery during the 1920's. Even after the League had stabilized Austria's currency by a special loan, the situation of the little republic remained precarious. Its industries, unable to sell their securities on a faltering market, relied to a dangerous extent on bank credits. When the world-wide depression began, Austria tottered on the edge of the gulf. Her Foreign Minister, Johann Schober, declared in September,

1930, that central Europe must have immediate relief, and that regional trade agreements offered the best hope. The resulting conference between the industrial nations of western Europe and the agricultural nations of eastern Europe, as we have noted, broke down. The areas east of the Rhine were left to face their thickening difficulties un-aided.

In the same month that Schober uttered his warning, an ominous danger signal came from Germany. Adolf Hitler's National Socialist Party, first appearing in the national elections in 1924, had that year obtained, under the proportional-repre-sentation system of voting, only thirty-two out of the nearly six hundred Reichstag seats. Later, the Nazi strength had fallen in 1928 to a mere dozen seats. But as the depression filled Germany with misery, the National Socialists in 1930 obtained 107 seats, and were well on their way to becoming the most powerful single party in the chamber, while at the other extreme the Communists also made sensational gains. The German Chancellor, Dr. Heinrich Bruening, issued emergency defla-tionary decrees, reducing interest rates, rents, cer-tain prices, and Government salaries. They failed to improve the situation. In both Austria and Germany, foreign investors grew uneasy and were briskly withdrawing their loans.

At this point, the Austrian and German Governments suddenly announced in March, 1931, a scheme for the formation of a customs union, which they declared was "destined to mark the beginning of a new order of European economic conditions on lines of regional agreements." They promised that the independence of the two countries would be rigidly maintained. But could they be believed? While it might be argued that a customs union would prove a first step toward that United States of Europe which Briand had proposed, the suspicious neighbors of Germany saw it rather as a step toward Pan-German union, and hence a violation of the treaty clauses of 1919 which had forbidden a German-Austrian *Anschluss*, or economic union.

The French Government immediately registered a formal protest, declaring that Austria contemplated an infraction of the Treaty of Saint-Germain. For Czechoslovakia, Foreign Minister Benes asserted that the customs union would injure European trade by raising the relatively low Austrian duties to the high German level, would force Austria to pay more for food and other commodities bought outside Germany, would reduce her export trade with non-German neighbors, would enable the powerful German industries to crush weak Austrian companies, and would not even profit German commerce materially, for Germany's sales to Austria had amounted to but 3 per cent of her total exports. The milk in the coconut, Benes declared, was political. An *Anschluss* between Germany and Austria really meant an organic union which would threaten the safety of all their neighbors.

By rallying her allies and bringing pressure on the League, France succeeded in halting the project. At the instance of the British, the League Council, on May 19, 1931, referred the question of a violation of the Treaty of Saint-Germain and the protocol of 1922 to the World Court. Austria, meanwhile, promised not to proceed with the scheme. Most French, Italians, Czechs, and Yugoslavs were bitterly opposed to the customs union; German and Austrian sentiment had been strongly enlisted in favor of it; while British opinion was neutral and conciliatory. In due course, the World Court gave its advisory opinion against the legality of the scheme. The net effect of the proposal had been to heighten the political antagonisms of the Continent.

But before the question went to the World Court, economic disaster struck Austria. The nation's largest bank, the Kredit-Anstalt, which controlled about three-fourths of the country's banking business and dominated the greater part of Austrian industry, had suffered heavily from mismanagement, the current depression, and threatening measures taken by French interests. Managers announced on May 11 that the bank's losses for 1930 had reached almost twenty million dollars, and that radical measures of relief were necessary to save it. The Government, the Austrian National Bank, and the Rothschilds, who had founded the institution in 1855, all promised to come to its rescue. But even their reassurances only briefly checked the run on deposits. The financial stability of Austria herself was endangered, and the industries of all the Succession States were threatened with a heavy blow.

America was directly affected by this, for Wall Street had loaned tremendous amounts to Germany. In the emergency, the Bank for International Settlements took hasty steps in late May to bring the central banks of France, Britain, Germany, Italy, and six other European nations, together with the Federal Reserve banks of the United States, into a consortium to sustain the Austrian institutions. At last, international cooperation on a broad scale, with American participation, was a reality. But France asked a price. She demanded the abandonment of the customs union. Bitter resentment at once spread throughout Germany and Austria over this attempt at political "blackmail," and the Austrian Government brusquely rejected the French demands. When Hoover learned of the French stipulations, he withdrew the assistance of the Federal Reserve; but

British opinion sympathized with Austria, and the Bank of England on June 16 stepped into the breach with a loan of $21,000,000.

Meanwhile, in these hectic days of May and June, 1931, Germany had become involved in the crisis; for the industrial expansion which she had enjoyed in 1924–28 had came to an abrupt end. Production, exports, and imports all fell off with disastrous suddenness. What capital did flow into Germany was of a short-term character, subject to rapid recall by creditors. As depression struck the country in 1929, tax receipts dropped sharply and the budget became painfully unbalanced. When on June 5, 1931, Chancellor Bruening issued his third emergency decree within a year, imposing higher taxes and requiring greater economies, and when immediately afterward he and Julius Curtius, the German Foreign Minister, arrived in England to talk with Prime Minister MacDonald, the whole world became worried over Germany's plight.

At this anxious moment President Hoover intervened. As early as May 1, he had decided that central Europe would have to be given help, and on May 6 had talked with the American Ambassador to Germany, home to report on the desperate situation. He had watched uneasily while the demands of panic-stricken foreign creditors drained from Germany a great part of her gold supply. By the end of the third week in June, the Reichsbank had lost more than two-fifths of its gold, or about $227,000,000. Of all the creditors Americans stood to lose most; they held considerably more than half of the long-term debt, and more than a third of the short-term obligations. A dam against the impending catastrophe had to be erected.

Hectic conferences took place in Washington and New York. The political correspondents in Washington reported that Owen D. Young, Parker Gilbert, George Harrison, and other leading financiers were pressing Hoover for action. Secretary Mellon and Under-Secretary Ogden Mills warned the President that the emergency had become critical. Finally, a piteous appeal arrived from President Von Hindenburg. "Relief must come at once if we are to avoid serious misfortune for ourselves and others," it ran. Early in June Hoover had a plan ready, and Stimson hailed it with delight—for Stimson always believed in bold leadership. Heartened by a Middle Western trip on which he was warmly cheered, the President determined to act. At the close of a Saturday afternoon, June 20, he made public his plan for meeting the world emergency. It was none too soon. "We have all been saying that the situation is quite like war," Stimson had written in his diary on June 15.

This was a proposal for a one-year moratorium on all intergovernmental debts. As matters stood, the Allies were expected to make debt payments in December, 1931, and June, 1932. These were to be postponed on condition that they gave Germany a twelve months' respite from reparations. Some of Hoover's advisers had urged a two or three-year breathing spell, but he feared the hostility of Congress. While the President made it clear that he was opposed to any cancellation of debts due the United States, he declared that his plan would give the next year "to the economic recovery of the world, and to help free the recuperative forces already in motion in the United States from retarding influences from abroad." A burst of American applause was loudly echoed in Britain and Germany, which with Austria and Italy at once indicated their complete approval. France, however, computing that the moratorium would cost her at least eighty million dollars, maintained an ominous silence.

Even if the plan could have been put into instant effect, it would probably have failed, for it came too late and offered too little. But deliberate French delays ruined all its slender chances of success. An aggrieved nationalism marked Gallic opinion and controlled the timid government. Paris remained firm in its objections day after day, so that it was not until July 5 that assiduous negotiations brought the United States, France, and Germany within sight of an agreement. Next day, July 6,

President Hoover cheerfully announced to the press that the moratorium agreement had been signed in Paris, and that its principles were accepted by all the creditor governments.

It had been signed, however, only after significant changes in favor of the French and their allies. Germany bound herself to make certain payments into the Bank for International Settlements. No barometer is more sensitive than that of finance, and it responded gloomily to the plain evidence of underlying Franco-German hatred and distrust. Paris financial houses led in exerting unfriendly pressure. The recall of short-term loans to Germany continued, the run on the German banks increased, and on July 13 one of the principal German banks failed. Next day, the Government closed all the banks of the Reich. The crisis had now reached a point of the utmost gravity to the world.

In a final effort to discover a way out, the British Government brought about a Seven-Power Conference. It decided that the great object was to halt the drain of short-term credits from Germany. In order to arrange a stoppage, the Bank for International Settlements called together a committee of financial experts. This committee, sitting in August, did end the drain by a "standstill agreement" for the continuance of existing short-term credits. Yet this furnished only a temporary respite. The most significant aspect of the Seven-

Power Conference and the committee sessions was the prominent part taken by American representatives. Two Cabinet members, Secretary Stimson and Secretary Mellon, who happened to be in Europe that summer, were appointed by Hoover to attend the conference—and as full delegates, not observers. The experts' committee chose for its chairman Albert H. Wiggin of the Chase National Bank of New York. America no longer pretended that it was not in the thick of international affairs.

Nothing, however, could halt the steady march of both America and Europe from a bad economic state to worse. Austria and Germany having been prostrated, proud Britain, so long financial mistress of the world, stood next in line. The standstill agreement simply increased the alarm of creditor groups the world over. It is not strange that they began to call in loans from all countries suspected of financial weakness. Britain, sustaining the pound at its pre-war level with inadequate reserves, was conspicuously one of these nations. Ever since the war, a pessimistic view of her economic future had been taken in many quarters. Even while the Seven-Power Conference was sitting in July, foreign balances were being withdrawn from the British banks. By the end of the month, the gold assets of the Bank of England had fallen below the 150 million pounds which a Government committee had declared the safe minimum reserve.

The possibility that Britain would be forced off gold now loomed up with frightening imminence. For a brief period, American and French banks joined hands to help sustain sterling. Unhappily, two ill-timed British papers, the Macmillan report on remedies for the economic situation and the May report on budgetary difficulties increased the international apprehension. Lord Macmillan's committee, pointing to the unfavorable balance of trade, declared that British manufacturing costs measured in gold were much too high as compared with foreign costs; and a considerable school of British opinion at once declared that abandonment of gold and adoption of a managed currency was the way out. Sir George May's committee pointed to an impending deficit and recommended cuts (the Labor members dissenting) in the social services. Appearing July 31, this report advertised to the world the grave budgetary situation of the country. More and more gold was withdrawn from Britain, and by August the Franco-American credit to help peg sterling was exhausted. Prime Minister MacDonald declared for a heavy reduction in social services, the dole, and Government salaries—whereupon the Labor Government split.

The upshot was the formation of a coalition ministry under MacDonald, the imposition of the cuts, a new loan by French and American bankers—and fresh trouble. The remedial measures proved futile to stay the flight from the pound. Labor opposition and a brief naval mutiny over pay reduction increased the uneasiness and the withdrawals. On September 20, 1931, when the British loss of gold since mid-July had reached a billion dollars, the Ministry decided to suspend the gold standard.

Where Britain led, other nations had to follow. Before a week had passed, the three Scandinavian nations dropped the gold standard, and Finland quickly joined the list. Most of South America was already off gold, and the autumn of 1931 found faith in the metal at the lowest ebb in human memory. From every quarter of the globe, meanwhile, came reports of deepening industrial depression, and of populations slipping into utter misery. Wall Street had fallen; the Kredit-Anstalt had fallen; the German financial system had fallen; even Britain had staggered.

In many parts of the world, alarmed people began to hoard currency. The credit system of the globe was breaking down. October witnessed a veritable gold panic in nearly all the highly industrialized nations. The United States would normally have been exempt, for almost nobody doubted the stability of the Federal Reserve System and the Treasury. But local bank failures in America had become distressingly numerous. They frightened depositors into hoarding their funds, and the banking structure was threatened with complete collapse. While various causes lay behind this banking weakness—bad management, the Wall Street slump, losses from the central European crisis, and sterling depreciation—the main factor was the fall in raw-material prices, which had bankrupted countless farmers, forced land to low values, and made mortgages uncollectible.

All these events formed the background of a dramatic event, the arrival of Prime Minister Pierre Laval of France in Washington for conversations with Hoover, which filled three October days. The slippery French lawyer had become premier in January, and was to retain power only four months longer. The main questions they had to discuss were the steps to be taken when the German moratorium ended, the maintenance of the gold standard, and the reduction of costly armaments. On the third point, no definite agreement was reached. On the second, the two nations made their position clear: they would sustain the gold standard as a major influence in the restoration of the normal economic life of the world. But it was on the sequels of the moratorium that the most important conclusions were announced. Hoover and Laval declared that before the year of postponement ended, some new agreement regarding intergovernmental debts might be necessary "covering the period of business depression," and that the initiative should be taken by the European powers chiefly concerned. From this statement was born the Lausanne Conference of the following year. And out of the Lausanne Conference was to come a new agreement for the reduction of the German reparations payments to a sum far below the level fixed in the Young Plan.

The Hoover-Laval conversations marked the highest point yet reached in America's progress toward genuine international action. Neither man had a firm grasp of the economic and financial realities of the day. Mr. Hoover's theory that foreign maladies offered the main reason why America did not rapidly recover has been rejected by all important economic analysts. Time proved Laval a mere jackal of politics, a cheap opportunist capable of treason. Yet here was a meeting which had far greater scope than the recent casual consultation of two American Cabinet members with European leaders on the salvation of the German banks; far greater scope than the discussions of the Wiggin Committee on a standstill agreement for Germany's short-term debt. It dealt with the fundamental problems of the globe. A stable basis for the world's currency, a world-wide reduction of armaments, a permanent settlement of the German reparations problem—these were objectives of the utmost importance. The conversations drove home to Americans the fact that their leaders must henceforth take a direct part in world affairs, for Europe

could never set her house in order without American aid, and a disordered European house meant
direful harm to the United States.

As 1931 ended, President Hoover, looking back
upon the cooperation of American and European
banks to meet the Central European and British
crises, upon his own conversations with Laval,
and upon the Government's partnership with the
League in preparing for a new disarmament conference, felt justified in pointing out that collabora-
tion was an established fact.

Yet it was inevitable that the next events should
widen the gulf which parted general American sentiment from other nations. Most Americans had
stubbornly declined to admit any connection between German reparations and the Allied debts to
the United States. Now, as the nations wrestled
with the economic tempest, both reparations and
debts were about to disappear together. When
they did, disillusionment and bitterness seized millions of citizens.

The Lausanne Conference, held in June, 1932,
was watched by Americans in two different tem-
pers. Never since 1920 had the differences between
isolationists and internationalists been more sharply etched. Such die-hards as Hiram Johnson, Burton
K. Wheeler, and Representative Martin Dies vocif-
erously insisted that the country, filled with its
own problems, had no business trying to aid alien

lands. Save the United States, not Europe; keep America for Americans; be generous at home before being generous abroad—so ran their injunctions. Congress, the House narrowly Democratic, the Senate narrowly Republican, showed a morose temper. It ratified the Hoover moratorium only after emitting a minatory growl: "It is hereby expressly declared to be against the policy of Congress that any of the indebtedness of foreign countries to the United States should be in any manner canceled or reduced." Yet a large section of American opinion, particularly in the East, was eager for a more generous treatment of the debt question, for it comprehended the folly of trying to collect obligations in full while erecting tariff barriers against foreign goods.

The official attitude of the Hoover Administration was quickly made clear. At heart Secretary Stimson was now a cancellationist, but he had to move cautiously. A note which he sent to the French Government laid down the thesis that the European powers should first work out their own settlement of the reparations issue, and then should come to the United States for a reexamination of the debt question. But they should come separately, not collectively. Although Washington reiterated its stale contention that no connection existed between debts and reparations, the implication that it might revise debts if the Allies revised reparations payments was a clear admission of the connection. This official Administration position did not harmonize with the statement just made by Congress. As a matter of fact, Hoover and Stimson were not in harmony. The President held that the war debts could be paid, while the Secretary was emphatically of the opinion that they could not.

The German Government _elt utterly unable to continue reparation payments. The Bruening Ministry also felt compelled to take a firm stand on the subject to meet the threat of the Communists on one side and the National Socialists on the other. When at the beginning of 1932 the British and French Governments offered to extend the moratorium for one year, Bruening flatly rejected the proposal. He insisted that no more payments whatever could be made by the Reich. Reparations were finished! As for short-term credits, the standstill agreement extended into 1933. The German elections that spring were watched by Europe with breathless interest. Voting on March 13 for the Presidency, the people gave Hindenburg, standing for reelection, 49.55 per cent of the ballots; Hitler 30.12 per cent; and Thaelmann, the Communist candidate, 13.23 per cent. In the ensuing run-off elections, Hindenburg received a clear majority, 53 per cent of the total. This seemed reassuring. The nation was not yet following the reckless leadership of the Nazis. But when the various states chose their Diets in March, a disquieting result appeared. In every state but Bavaria, the Nazis obtained a plurality, and in the most important state, Prussia, they won 162 of the 422 seats. They had obtained a dominating position, for while they could not govern alone, no government could be set up without accepting their terms.

Politically, Germany's foot was set upon a slippery road. So violent were the party antagonisms that civil war seemed at hand. Hindenburg, in desperation, on May 30 forced the Bruening Ministry out of power, and gave the Chancellorship to the stupid Franz von Papen, who was ready to play into Hitler's hands. Meanwhile, the French people had turned decisively to the left, placing Edouard Herriot in power.

The reparations settlement reached at Lausanne constituted a recognition that the old order was indeed dead. After much negotiation, the Allies agreed to accept a final payment of about $715,-000,000; but even this was to be made in Government bonds to be deposited in the Bank for International Settlements, and to be sold only when the economic position of Germany rendered it possible. Little hope existed that they could be disposed of in the near future. As a matter of fact, they were never sold. Bruening had been right; reparations were ended. Had the fact been admitted before the German elections, and had other concessions been made to him, the fatal rise of the Nazis to power might have been avoided.

But if reparations were dead, what of the war debts? At Lausanne that thorny question was covered by a "gentlemen's agreement" among the British, French, Italian, and Belgian representatives which declared, in effect, that ratification of the new reparations scheme would not be effected by the four powers "until a satisfactory settlement has been reached between them and their own creditors." Inevitably, this aroused great resentment in the United States. President Hoover was so irritated that he wished to issue a denunciatory statement; and even after Stimson had expostulated with him for three days he felt it necessary to publish a defiant letter to Chairman Borah of the Senate Foreign Relations Committee, saying that American policies would not be influenced by any foreign combination. Of course, the gentlemen's agreement was maladroit. But actually it represented that same clear-eyed facing of realities that was implicit in the reparations agreement. The debts, too, were dead. As a matter of fact, France, Belgium, and Poland defaulted on their debt installment in December, 1932. The British, who were bearing much the heaviest burden, used their slender gold reserves that month to send over their full sum of $96,000,000. Italy, Czechoslovakia, Finland, and two of the Baltic states also paid their installments, which altogether amounted to only $3,000,000.

This was almost the end. The world was already experiencing fresh economic shocks. In the United States, the winter of 1932–33, following Franklin D. Roosevelt's victory over Hoover, was the blackest depression period in the nation's history. The suffering in Germany, when Hitler took power in January, 1933, was agonizing. In June, 1933, the British sent a token payment of $10,000,000 on their debt, and four other nations sent small sums. Then, after the passage of the Johnson Act, which stigmatized even partial payments as a default, all receipts ceased. Under the *letter* of the post-war agreements, the United States was to have received about $22,000,000,000 in interest and principal, just as the Allies were to have recovered vast sums from Germany, and just as Britain was to have collected whatever part of her $10,000,000,-000 loans to her fighting partners she needed to repay America. Altogether, about $50,000,000,000 was to have changed hands. Now all this had to be given up. Britain had obtained perhaps one-tenth of her $10,000,000,000 in loans, and the United States received only a little over one-tenth of the $22,000,000,000 on which it had once counted.

It was now easy to see what well-informed economists like John Maynard Keynes had known from the beginning—that the debt and reparations payments anticipated in 1920 were impossible. They became thrice impossible when the United States insisted on a heavy export surplus in foreign trade, rejecting any large shipments of goods from the debtor nations, and when French policies denied Germany and Austria free scope for recovery. In the United States, nevertheless, the feeling remained widespread that default was deliberate and dishonest. Plain citizens, meeting their own heavy tax bills, and not realizing that international payments can in the last analysis be made only in goods and services, believed that they had been cheated by fraudulent foreign governments. Resentment was freely expressed, and was long sustained. It played a part in the sentiment which supported Franklin D. Roosevelt's initial measures of economic nationalism. As the world storm grew fiercer, the disposition to retreat within America's historic shell of self-regard increased.

"Never in history," said Ogden Mills to Stimson in 1932, "have the American people been so isolationist as now."

Yet some lessons were being learned. One of Hoover's last official utterances was a solemn warning against a continuance of the economic warfare that now seemed all too likely to ravage the entire globe. For two years, he said on February 12, 1933, the crash of one foreign nation after another had made the economic firmament tremble. The nations "have in turn sought to protect themselves by erecting barriers, until today, as a result of such financial breakdown, we are in the presence of an incipient outbreak of economic war in the world. We will be ourselves forced to defensive action to protect ourselves unless this mad race is stopped. We must not be the major victim of it all." Out of a deep sense of the purblind folly of this warfare was soon to be born Secretary Hull's attempt at a partial liberation of international trade by reciprocal trade agreements.

CHAPTER VI

JAPAN DEFIES THE WORLD

UPON his retirement in 1933, Secretary Stimson wrote: "I believe that important foundations of progress have been laid, upon which it will be possible for an enduring structure to be erected by the labors of our successors." He referred to the happy understanding achieved with Britain following Rapidan and the London Naval Conference, to the success of the Hoover Administration in improving relations with Latin America, and to its increased cooperation with the League. He might well take pride in his labors. Unfortunately, these solid achievements were largely offset by the worrisome questions bequeathed to Franklin D. Roosevelt: the debris of war debts and reparations; the high tariffs, unstabilized currencies, and other impediments to world trade; the still unsolved problem of reducing land and air armaments; and, in the Far East, the defiance of Japan. Of all the foreign difficulties of the early 1930's, those with Japan were the most profoundly disturbing.

American attention in 1930–34 was naturally centered upon the domestic scene. But men could not fail to observe that international affairs were deteriorating. These were the years of Japan's unchecked invasion of Manchuria, the breakdown of the World Economic Conference, and the failure of the forty-nation Disarmament Conference. They were the years in which the Nazis seized power and Hitler consolidated his dictatorship over the Third Reich. Millions of Americans became convinced that the Old World was hopeless, that new wars were in the making, and that self-containment was the watchword of American safety. This current of opinion might have been altered had Hoover and Roosevelt pursued an aggressively internationalist course. But urgent home problems took precedence, and although Secretaries Stimson and Cordell Hull were anxious to promote international action, both Hoover and after him Roosevelt were determined to run no risks that would interfere with domestic recovery.

It was Japanese action which first struck the tocsin of danger; action the more shocking because, despite Japan's record of aggressive expansion from 1895 to 1920, it was generally unexpected. Ever since the fall of the Shogunate in 1867, Japan had witnessed a series of oscillations between military and liberal leadership. The military had been in the saddle during the First World War. Then in the 1920's parliamentarism and peace seemed gaining greater authority than ever before. The army and navy were held in subordination to civilian chieftains; particularly after 1924, Cabinets representative of the Diet majority were chosen; the two principal parties, the Seiyukai and the Minseito, kept in fair balance; and liberal reforms were introduced, the chief being a universal manhood suffrage law (1925). Such leaders as Korekiyo Takahashi in finance and Baron Kijuru Shidehara in foreign affairs were men of vision who staunchly opposed militarist tendencies. Shidehara, after signing the Nine-Power Treaty, was steadfast in supporting a policy of friendship toward the Chinese.

Yet as the decade closed, certain ominous events occurred. In 1927–29 a reactionary Prime Minister, General Baron Tanaka, obtained power. A big, burly soldier, with a flair for politics, he was bent on expansion and foreign adventure. After a military demonstration in Shantung to try to check the advance of Kuomintang forces into northern China, he turned toward Manchuria. In June, 1927, he brought about a "Far Eastern Conference," the precise decisions of which have been a theme of endless controversy. No official statement of findings was ever issued. What is certain is that military leaders demanded a thoroughgoing occupation of Manchuria and Mongolia and that a radical new policy was determined upon—to be pushed as soon as public sentiment was ready.

Later the Chinese published the "Tanaka Memorial," which they alleged gave the main conclusions of the conference. This memorial, covering wide ground, declared that Japan must adopt a policy of blood and iron. "In the future, if we want to control China, we must first crush the United States . . . but in order to conquer China we must first conquer Manchuria and Mongolia. In order to conquer the world we must first conquer China. . . . Then the world will realize that Eastern Asia is ours, and will not dare to violate our rights." The authenticity of the document was always stubbornly denied by the Japanese Government; but though expert observers doubted that Prime Minister Tanaka would have signed so dangerous a paper, they also agreed that it probably represented militarist opinion at the conference.

The situation in chaotic China offered Japan tempting opportunities. In 1926 the Southern Government had definitely emerged to leadership in creating a true Chinese nation. Its gifted chieftain Sun Yat-sen, who died in 1925, was replaced by a still more extraordinary man, a former commandant of the Whampoa military academy named Chiang Kai-shek. His forces made steady progress. By the end of 1926 the Southern armies held the

lower valley of the Yangtse, occupying Hupeh;
and on New Year's Day in 1927, Chiang executed
a memorable stroke by a proclamation transferring
his capital to Hankow. He was shortly deposed
from his post as Commander-in-Chief, but he at
once (April, 1927) set up an opposition Kuomintang or National Government at Nanking. Late in
the year he married Mei-ling Soong (an American-
educated woman of talents as unusual as his own,
the sister of Finance Minister T. V. Soong and of
Mrs. Sun Yat-sen) and was restored to his post as
Commander-in-Chief. In midsummer of 1928 he,
with two other National commanders, was able to
stage a ceremony in the Western Hills at Peking
in which they announced to the spirit of Sun Yat-
sen their consolidation of China. For a brief moment Chiang's prospects for bringing the republic
into a state of passable unity and tranquility
seemed bright; but civil strife never really ceased.

As Chinese turmoil and disintegration persisted,
the aggressive Baron Tanaka wished to make the
most of them. In his eagerness he quickly over-
reached himself. He induced a section of the press
to begin beating the tom-toms for expansion. Manchuria, a land of vast resources, had about 30 million Chinese and about a million Japanese subjects,
most of them Koreans. He inspired Japanese intrigues to create a state of disorder in the province.
In June, 1928, however, the assassination of the

Manchurian war lord Chang Tso-lin struck the foundations from under Tanaka's Ministry. Chang had been mortally wounded by bombs exploded under his railroad carriage at Mukden, and everyone knew that Japanese army officers were responsible. No impartial investigation of Chang's assassination was permitted. But so outrageous an act could not fail to horrify all Japanese liberals. Critics in Tokyo pointed out that the Japanese army was responsible for order in the Mukden area; they demanded punishment of those responsible. Reports had to be made to the throne. At length, as the agitation continued, Baron Tanaka had to resign (July, 1929), and the pandemonium which had marked Diet discussions died away. An eminent liberal, Yuko Hamaguchi, became Prime Minister, and Baron Shidehara took charge again of the Foreign Office. Once more a peaceful parliamentarian government was in full power. To emphasize the enlightened character of the new Ministry, the Portfolio of War was given to General Ugaki, a man of relatively liberal views.

Underneath the surface, however, the currents were beginning to run against liberalism. By autumn of 1929, Japan felt the grip of low prices and falling trade. The silk market was hard hit, and the Smoot-Hawley Tariff soon completed its ruin. Bankruptcies, unemployment, and rising taxes bred general discontent, and the leaders in power suffered. Japan's rapid transformation from a hermit medieval state into a modern industrial nation had fostered a dismaying increase in population. The birth rate was at an "Oriental" figure; while the death rate, thanks to the rapid adoption of Western sanitation and medicine, fell to Occidental levels. By 1932 the annual increase exceeded a million. Even conservative estimates indicated that Japan's total population would reach nearly 80 millions by 1950. What could be done to sustain it? The only way out was by extension of the economic frontier, and to many leaders this seemed also to imply a broad extension of political frontiers.

Another unhappy element was the growing disillusionment with parliaments and politicians. Democracy had never been more than a façade in Japan, and the façade was beginning to crash. The disorders of the Diet in 1927–28, the fierce exchange of invective between the two main parties, the evidence that great industrial combinations like the Mitsui and Mitsubishi dominated many political leaders, and the proofs of abundant corruption, all aroused disgust with the governmental system. Many people demanded the discipline of a military regime. At any rate, there seemed little to choose between military domination and industrial exploitation. Above all, with the fall of Tanaka the militarists realized that they must take desperate measures or lose everything. Against naval opposition, Hamaguchi determinedly carried through the London Conference treaty arranged at the beginning of 1930, while in China the Kuomintang ascendancy was now established beyond all hope of dislodgment, and in Manchuria "the Young Marshal," Chang Tso-lin's son, had recognized the Kuomintang Government and made it clear that he would resist Japanese encroachments. The militarists must strike, or they would lose all their aims.

The first step of the military party was to get rid of Prime Minister Hamaguchi and War Minister Ugaki. In the fall of 1930 a young man shot the Prime Minister, who never really recovered and died within a year. One of Japan's truly great leaders, of clear brain, honest heart, and steadfast courage, he had been a pillar of democracy who could not be replaced. Meanwhile, Ugaki, after months of illness, was compelled by ill health to resign. The death of Hamaguchi and disappearance of Ugaki cleared the way for the Manchurian adventure. A new Cabinet took power; its strongest single figure was the new War Minister, Jiro Minami, a young general who believed in ruthless territorial expansion.

Within six months after the new Ministry took power, the army was ready to begin its conquest of Manchuria. Behind it stood many businessmen, for the Japanese investment in China, including Manchuria, was by 1931 put at about $1,500,000,-000. The various holdings in Manchuria constituted a rich stake. Even liberal leaders believed that the island empire should have railroad rights, a free opportunity to widen its investment in Manchurian industries, and guarantees of safety for the many Koreans and Japanese in the area. In trying to make sure of these objects, the Japanese found the Chinese Nationalists resisting them by boycotts against Japanese products, and by attacks upon many vested Japanese interests. Hostility between Japan and China, which was of long standing, had in fact become very troublesome. The Manchurian railway treaties constituted one of the sore spots, and a year or two earlier might well have claimed League attention as a minor dispute with grave potentialities.

The "Mukden incident" of the night of September 18, 1931, was the first step in the proposed conquest. On the ground that a few yards of the South Manchuria Railway had been torn up by Chinese soldiers, the Japanese set in motion a preconceived scheme for occupation. So well had army leaders planned their move that by dawn next day their troops were occupying every strategic center in the Mukden area. Within a few weeks every point in which the Japanese were interested had been taken. Bombing of the defenseless population of Chinchow and other centers horrified the Western world. Baron Shidehara seemed completely helpless against the military. The Japanese movement was one of the events which, along with the deepening of the depression and the solidification of American isolationism, made 1931 seem to Arnold Toynbee the *annus terribilis* of the post-war period.

America was quick to act. On September 22, Secretary Stimson told the Japanese Ambassador that the seizure of South Manchuria raised grave issues with respect to the Nine-Power Treaty and the Kellogg Pact. That same day the League Council sent notes urging China and Japan to withdraw their troops from the area of conflict and to avoid any provocative act. The Chinese Government had made a formal appeal to the League under Article XI. Secretary Stimson believed that the League was the proper agent for handling the situation and thought that the United States and the League should collaborate closely; he saw to it that Hugh Wilson, Minister at Berne, established relations with the chief Council members, including Robert Cecil. On September 25, Stimson sent Nanking and Tokyo notes of the same purport as the League's. On October 5 he went further, urging the League, through our Consul in Geneva, to exert all its pressure to control the action of China and Japan. The American Government, promised Stimson, would "endeavor to reinforce what the League does," and make clear its keen interest in seeing the Kellogg-Briand Pact and Nine-Power Treaty respected. At the same time, the State Department took the view that it would be wise to support the liberal Shidehara by patience and reticence, giving him an opportunity to regain control, if he could, over the military men.

This was unquestionably the moment for vigorous and concerted action. It was in fact one of the most fateful moments in modern history. Japan was still relatively vulnerable; Britain and America had free hands, neither yet fearful of Germany. Why did the Western powers not act with resolute decision? The reasons are complex; and they make it clear that the times were unpropitious for anything beyond an experiment in conciliation. If the statesmen of 1931 could have foreseen the future, they *would* have acted with vigor against Japan. The actual circumstances, however, made hesitation all too natural.

England was facing a general election, which took place on October 27. Stanley Baldwin's business-minded National Government was asking for a new mandate, and could not foresee that it would win a tremendous majority. In the United States, public opinion was moving strongly against the Hoover Administration. Moreover, October was a singularly confused month. It saw Hoover holding

conferences with the leaders of both parties to discuss the world's financial crisis; Premier Laval of
France journeying to Washington to raise the question of war debts and reparations; the Foreign
Minister of Italy laying plans to follow him; Chancellor Bruening forming a new Ministry; and the
Cortes in Madrid deciding that Church and State
should be separated. The American budget was
sagging under a two-billion-dollar deficit, in itself
a great barrier to boldness of action. Germany was
facing financial collapse. Parliament was about to
be asked to enact the Statute of Westminster,
registering the momentous conclusions of the Imperial Conference as to Dominion independence.
Finally, large conservative groups the world over
regarded Tokyo's action complacently. In particular, many people in the Dutch East Indies, Australia, and New Zealand showed actual relief when
the aggressive Japanese engaged themselves in the
Manchurian adventure. Nippon would not turn
southward! Business interests from Boston to San
Francisco, and from London to Calcutta, felt no
appetite for foreign risks.

What ensued, then, was a series of procrastinat-
ing, evasive, and futile steps. The League Council,
with Briand as President and Lord Reading making his first appearance as British Foreign Minister, had taken up the crisis in the closing days
of September. At its invitation (October 16), the

American Consul in Geneva sat with it, but under strict instructions from Washington to take no part save when application of the Kellogg Pact was discussed. Five members of the Council promptly reminded Japan of her obligations under the Kellogg Pact, and the United States followed suit. The Japanese replied that the dispute must be settled by direct negotiations between China and Japan, and intimated that the forces occupying Chinese towns would have to remain, pending the settlement of "fundamental principles." The League Council then, on October 24, passed a resolution asking Japan to withdraw her troops by November 16 to points within the railway zone. After some delay, on November 5, the State Department informed Tokyo that it supported the spirit of the League resolution, and definitely regarded Japan's course as an infraction of the Nine-Power Treaty and Kellogg Pact. Stimson's policy, as he has told us, was to avoid public statements critical of Japan, so as not to embarrass Shidehara, while simultaneously expressing through diplomatic channels the strong American concern over the aggressive acts of the Japanese Government.

But Japan's position remained one of defiance. China was obstructing her just claims in Manchuria, she argued, and until they were granted, she could not withdraw. The Japanese militarists contended that civil strife, banditry, and misgovernment, with the rapid growth of anti-Japanese feeling, made a restoration of order imperative. Instead of contracting troop operations, they steadily advanced their forces, ostensibly to guard railways and repair bridges. Puppet authorities were being set up under Japanese protection. The Council met again in Paris on November 16, the date set for complete withdrawal. When that date arrived, Japan was rapidly putting an end to all authority of the Chinese Republic in South Manchuria. Danger existed that the conflict would spread till Soviet Russia was involved, and half of Asia ablaze. What would the Council and the United States do?

Rigorous action would have meant serious danger of war, and this risk neither the United States nor the principal League powers were prepared to run. President Hoover knew that American opinion would not support a conflict to preserve Chinese authority over Manchuria. The land was too remote, the national stake in it too small. From his Far Eastern experience as a mining engineer he had drawn a firm belief that the sheer massive weight of the Chinese population would enable it to resist any attack and absorb any invader; for he did not realize that new mechanisms of military control had been invented. In a memorandum laid before his Cabinet in October, he spoke harshly of Japanese offenses, but added: "These acts do not impair the freedom of the American people, the economic or moral future of the people. I do not propose ever to sacrifice American life for anything short of this . . . we will not go along on war or any of the sanctions either military or economic, for these are the roads to war." This statement, reflecting majority sentiment, largely tied the hands of Secretary Stimson. For that matter, Stimson agreed with Hoover that the League ought not to be allowed to deposit the baby on the American doorstep.

It is true that Japan was vulnerable, for her economic life was more largely dependent on foreign trade than that of any other great nation save Britain. More than a third of this trade was with the United States. The chief Japanese export, raw silk, was almost completely taken by America, while from the United States Japan bought 40 per cent of the raw cotton that she made into cloth to sell to her own people, to China, and to India. An American import-export embargo might almost ruin Japan even if no other nation acted. But the injury would have been reciprocal.

Then, too, America had neglected its navy, whereas Japan had built her fleet up to full treaty strength; so that if Japan were pushed to desperation, the United States stood in a perilous position. No new battleships or heavy cruisers were constructed, of course, during 1922–32. The Washington treaty had set a maximum of ten thousand tons and eight-inch guns on future cruisers. In 1924, Congress had authorized eight cruisers of slightly over nine thousand tons, two of which were started at once, and the other six in 1927. This program gave the country about 55,000 tons of new scout cruisers with 74 eight-inch guns. A second program for an airplane carrier and fifteen scout cruisers (later reduced to ten by the London Conference of 1931) was authorized in 1929, but the first of them were not delivered until 1934. Only in the development of the naval air service was satisfactory progress made. The Naval Bill of 1926 authorized a strength of a thousand planes, which was reached by 1930. By 1932 the naval air service was by far the world's largest, and in personnel was double the size of the Japanese service. But elsewhere the fleet was weak and ill-balanced. The Japanese, meanwhile, had been building four large cruisers that were almost certainly over treaty limits, and had also probably begun to violate the treaty clauses which forbade the construction of naval bases.

Authoritative figures tell their own story—and help explain American caution in the Far Eastern crisis. In the dozen years 1920–32, the United States had built 40 ships of 197,640 tons; Japan had built 104 ships of 410,467 tons. At the close of 1932 the American and Japanese fleets were almost precisely equal in size. Of under-age vessels

the United States had 101, with 728,050
tons; Japan had 184, with 726,138 tons. The
American merchant marine had also sunk into
decay.

Nor were the two chief European powers any
readier than Hoover for war. Had Briand remained
in power, France might have responded energet-
ically to this first great test of the pact to which
he had given his name. Unhappily, he had been
supplanted by Laval and other unprincipled men.
The Quai d'Orsay, more fearful of Russian Communism than of Japan, accepted Tokyo's repre-
sentation of herself as "the great bastion against
the onslaughts of Muscovite darkness." As for
Britain, her representative in Tokyo, Sir Francis
Lindley, sent home reports which shocked fellow
diplomats by their bias in favor of Japanese aims.
At the Foreign Office, Lord Reading was replaced
in November, 1931, by the agile Sir John Simon,
who knew that business circles were anxious not
to offend Japan, and that many exporters expected
foreign trade to profit if the Japanese gave direction to "backward" and "chaotic" China. Time
proved that Simon might have done well to make
the most of Stimson's proposals, supporting his
suggestion that the League apply economic sanctions. If, despite the many reasons for hesitation,
he had stood firm on principle, this bold acceptance
of risks would perhaps have yielded golden returns

to the League and the world. Unfortunately, the complexities of the situation impressed him. Sir John remembered the Russian menace; he recalled the old Japanese alliance and Japan's help against Germany in 1914. Undoubtedly, he also heard from his American agents that Hoover and American opinion were not behind Stimson, and that the United States would run no risk of war. Stimson himself, while delighted at the thought of League sanctions, was opposed to any American sanctions; not, he later admitted, a noble position. In Lloyd George's phrase, Simon had sat so long on the fence that the iron had entered into his soul, and a cynical, timid, shortsighted practicality governed his decisions. But the United States, too, was for sitting on the fence; everyone concerned, as Stimson writes, wanted Japan checked, but wanted somebody else to do it.

The new meeting of the Council, held in Paris in November, 1931, therefore ended not in action but investigation. General Dawes, American Ambassador in London, crossed the Channel to be present for consultation. Dawes knew finance much better than international affairs; he had to be taught everything, and one Swiss observer wrote that "a volume could be filled with anecdotes to which his ignorance gave rise." The Council, conducting its business chiefly in private meetings, soon attained the grand object of doing something impressive

without running any risk of conflict. All idea of
requiring Japanese evacuation by a fixed date was
given up. So was the early demand for a flat statement that evacuation must precede the Chino-
Japanese negotiation on treaty rights. So was the
request for delimitation of a neutral zone between
the two armies. With Japan assenting, a resolution
was adopted on December 10 for a neutral investi-
gating commission (such as China had requested
two and a half months earlier!) under the League
aegis, to visit the Far East and report on the whole
range of disputes between Japan and China. Five
men were shortly appointed, one an American,
General Frank McCoy; and they chose the able
Lord Lytton as chairman.

That this course was of doubtful utility was
plain at the time. Investigation on the spot could
discover little that was not already known. The
delay precisely suited the Japanese militarists, who
hastened to complete their occupation of Manchuria before the League could take adverse steps.
Worst of all, the appointment of the Commission
confused world opinion. The vital issue was the
brutal violence of Japan's conquest of Manchuria
and the plain breach of treaties. An effort had been
made in the League Covenant and the Kellogg
Pact to establish international relations on a basis
of ethics, reason, and the renunciation of force.
Japan had arbitrarily attacked this basis, with all

that it meant to the hope of future peace, and had brazenly widened her breach. Action, not investigation, was needed.

If the action taken by the League verged on futility, so did the course pursued by Washington. The United States was unwilling on the one hand to condone Japanese aggression, and unready on the other to stop it by economic or military measures. What then *would* it do? It turned to the Hoover-Stimson doctrine of non-recognition. Rejecting steps which might lead to war, President Hoover on November 19 suggested to Stimson that the American Government announce that it would not recognize or consent to any treaty made under armed compulsion. The Secretary at once warmed to this idea that the United States should never treat as legal any gains made by aggression. He keenly appreciated the special trust in American friendship which had been built up in China by Hay's Open Door policy and by generations of effort on the part of American missionaries, teachers, and doctors. It would be tragic if the United States now allowed the Chinese people to conclude that, after so long laboring to protect Chinese sovereignty and promote Chinese well-being, Washington was turning its back on the Far East and allowing a brutal and rapacious power to pillage and destroy as it pleased. The non-recognition doctrine would at least express the deep moral concern of the United States for China, and its stern condemnation of Japanese attacks. On January 7, 1932, therefore, Secretary Stimson sent the Japanese and Chinese Governments a note which declared that America could not recognize any treaty or agreement which impaired the independence or integrity of China, or infringed upon the Open Door policy. What was more, the United States "does not intend to recognize any situation, treaty, or agreement which may be brought about by means contrary to the covenants and obligations of the Pact of Paris. . . ."

This had a brave ring—but little or no practical effect. The Japanese paid no real attention to it. Indeed, they insolently thanked the United States for the support it gave to Japan's efforts to defend the sanctity of treaties! Washington expected the adherence of Sir John Simon, and should have had it; but Simon rebuffed Stimson by formally expressing his confidence in Japan's desire to respect the Open Door. France, Holland, and Italy also declined to follow the American lead. The moral weight of the Hoover-Stimson doctrine would have been greatly enhanced by cordial European support. As it was, the non-recognition doctrine failed to deter the Japanese in the slightest; it was a fillip on the wrist which they disregarded. Its only utility lay in keeping the American record straight, in appealing on moral grounds to world opinion, and in giving some slight encouragement to the hard-pressed Chinese.

Encouraged by Occidental weakness, the Japanese militarists on January 28, 1932, suddenly struck at Shanghai. This, the greatest of Chinese commercial centers, had large American, British, French, Italian, and Japanese communities living under their own laws and policed by their own forces; the foreign area was a thickly populated district of more than twelve square miles. The new blow was delivered by the navy, which was jealous of army successes. The Japanese Consul-General had sent the Mayor of Greater Shanghai an ultimatum demanding the suppression of anti-Japanese associations, with other measures; and although the Mayor returned a satisfactory reply, the Japanese Admiral took the law into his own hands by sending marines into the water-front district of Chapei. Bloody fighting followed. Part of the city was fired, thousands of civilian refugees perished under cruel bomb attacks, and as the battle continued, army forces were landed. After brave resistance, the Chinese were compelled to negotiate an armistice. Once more China appealed to the League Council (February 9, 1932), and an Assembly meeting was called for March 3.

Events were plainly outrunning the Lytton Report. But would the League really act? Would the United States, with Stimson ready to bluff about sanctions but Hoover totally unwilling to use them, take any forward step? Newton D. Baker, President Lowell of Harvard, and other prominent men were arguing vigorously that the United States and Geneva should cooperate in imposing economic sanctions, but with a limited public response. Stimson proposed to the British Government in February that it and Washington issue a joint declaration that the Kellogg Pact and Nine-Power Treaty were fully binding; and he held five transatlantic telephone conversations with Sir John Simon to discuss this in detail—the first important use of the transatlantic telephone in foreign relations. Simon approved of the plan in principle, but in practice he held back—arguing that Britain must wait on the League.

In the end both America and the League contented themselves with measured, impressive, and purely academic rebukes. Stimson on February 23 sent Senator Borah a long letter (his most important state paper, he later wrote) condemning Japan, expressing the deep sentiment of the United States for the orderly and peaceful development of the four hundred million Chinese people, recalling the solemn pledges of the Nine-Power Treaty, and reiterating at length his non-recognition doctrine. An eloquent and impressive document, the letter created a sensation both in America and in Europe. The League Council had already (February 16) issued an appeal to Japan which called attention to her engagements under the Nine-Power Treaty, and which implied adoption of the non-recognition doctrine. On March 11—at the instance of Sir John Simon—the League Assembly reenunciated the Hoover-Stimson doctrine in emphatic terms. But Japan cared little whether her occupation of Manchuria was recognized so long as no forcible interference took place. Ten days before the League pronouncement, the generals had set up their puppet state of Manchukuo. All the earlier assurances regarding ultimate Japanese evacuation of points outside the railway zone were now forgotten as Tokyo took the stand that the "nationalist" movement, bought and paid for, must be kept under her protection.

In blood-stained Shanghai the Japanese did shortly recede. The conflict there had been marked by two dramatic developments. One was the impressive reaction of world opinion against Japan; the other was the unexpectedly effective resistance of the heroic Nineteenth Route Army. Hostilities ceased just as the Assembly, by unanimous vote, came as close to condemning Japan as an aggressor as it could, without using that word. The Lytton Commission reached Shanghai at this moment, receiving a rapturous welcome as a symbol of world help. During the spring of 1932 the Japanese forces were withdrawn. The spokesman for the Tokyo

Foreign Office, in announcing this (May 11), attributed the decision to his Government's wish, by yielding to international opinion, to "end the world-wide odium which has fallen upon" Japan; and Stimson remained hopeful that similar action would be taken in Manchuria.

Actually, the Nipponization of the northern province steadily continued. Tokyo gave formal recognition to the puppet state on September 15, 1932, immediately concluding an alliance with it. That, in Japanese eyes, closed the affair. With defiant mien, the Japanese Ambassador told Stimson early in 1933 that no compromise on the Manchurian question was possible, and no further meddling with Japan's position would be tolerated. Next month, on February 24, the League Assembly adopted the Lytton Report. It was a statesmanlike document, thorough and accurate in its analysis of the situation, and while courageous in condemning Japanese aggression, yet honest in acknowledging that this had grown out of a complex set of unhappy conditions in China and Manchuria. It wisely tried to show Japan that a better course existed than the imposition of a permanent hegemony upon thirty million Chinese, proposing that by direct negotiations, under international auspices, China and Japan should agree upon a comprehensive settlement. This settlement should include provincial autonomy for Manchuria under

Chinese sovereignty, with numerous foreign advisers, many of them Japanese; full protection of Japanese and Korean minorities and their property rights; and a Chino-Japanese trade treaty, forbidding boycotts. Next day Stimson informed the Secretary-General that the American Government agreed with the League's action. March of 1933 found Japan giving formal notice of withdrawal from Geneva.

There had been two moments when drastic action might have brought Japan to a standstill—or to war. The first was in November, 1931, when the League Council met in Paris to find that Tokyo had not withdrawn its troops within the time limit assigned. If America, Britain, and the League had then come out for bold economic and financial measures, and had made overtures to enlist Russia, Japan would have been in an awkward predicament. An embargo on credits and raw materials would have hit the Empire hard. The second opportunity came when the League Assembly met on March 3, 1932. Fifty nations were represented. They made it clear that practically the whole planet condemned Japan's course. Many small countries were eager to vindicate the League by a formal decision that Japan had violated the Covenant, and the application of economic sanctions under Article XVI. It was the great powers which recoiled because they knew that if Japan fought back, as a cornered panther fights, they would have to accept the perils. The first opportunity to bring Japan sharply to terms was missed when the nations turned to the Lytton investigation; the second was side-stepped when they deemed it sufficient to slap Japan on the wrist with the Stimson doctrine.

In reviewing this chronicle of half-measures and cross-purposes, it would be a signal error to lay the heaviest blame upon President Hoover, Sir John Simon, the French Foreign Minister, or other leaders. Public opinion was primarily at fault—the people themselves. In all countries feeling was divided on the Japanese problem. Immersed in their terrible home problems, with want on every street corner and ruin in every headline, the Western democracies had little leisure to realize what the far-off Manchurian quarrel portended. Not one American in a hundred believed that Manchuria was worth the bones of an Iowa farm lad.

Since the cockatrice's egg went unsmashed, the serpent emerged and grew. In Japan the militarists now exulted in their power. War Minister Miniami knew that his nominal chiefs would be powerless to check him. It was true that Baron Wakatsuki, a believer in parliamentary institutions and hater of militarism, was Prime Minister; true that Baron Shidehara, a true friend of China and of treaty obligations, was Foreign Minister. But while these men held *office*, the army and navy chiefs held *power*. The two Ministers might have resigned. Instead, they remained, and Shidehara not only defended so far as he could the militarists' iniquities, but misled the Western powers by promises of evacuation which the generals ignored. Why? Perhaps because of a mistaken belief that patriotism demanded national unity, because he could not provoke an internal rupture when the country was meeting an external crisis, and because he thought that if he stayed in office he might moderate the army's ambitions. At any rate, two successive Cabinets of predominately liberal tendencies yielded ground, and long before the second left office, the Manchurian adventure had scored a complete victory for aggression. The evil growth of militarism put down new banyan roots.

Conditions in China itself continued distressing. The Communist power now emerged into plain view, a disruptive influence destined to play a tremendous role during the next fifteen years. The Russian Government had been quick to see the possibilities offered by Chinese poverty, ignorance, and discontent. As early as 1920 the Comintern had sent an agent into China to set up Communist units and publish a magazine. The formal organization of the Chinese Communist Party had taken place at Shanghai on July 1, 1921, and new Russian agents had been dispatched to help form branches.

For some time the CCP, under instructions from the Comintern, had followed a policy of "parasitism" by attaching itself to the Kuomintang. Annual congresses were held, of which the sixth took place not in China but in Moscow.

Gradually the Communists grew in vigor and did their utmost to undermine the authority of Chiang Kai-shek and his lieutenants. Then in 1931 they seized the dark hour of the Japanese invasion to set up their new Communist Republic. It had its own government, army, laws, and currency. The result was that Chiang, instead of being able to devote his whole energy to resistance against the Japanese, had to undertake a series of campaigns against this Soviet Republic, operating from its mountain-protected capital at Kangsi. His movements were ultimately successful, and he forced the Chinese Communists to retreat six thousand miles into the northwest. But as they retreated they laid waste a great swath of Chinese territory, and they set up a new center in the western province of Shensi, which already had a large Communist element. Here they presented a fresh menace to Chinese unity. The division of Chinese energies in the face of Japanese aggression was highly unfortunate.

While Japan was taking the path of aggression, America turned to retreat in the Philippines. With motives derived in part from the desire of American sugar and other interests to escape Filipino competition, and in part from a wish to get rid of embarrassing commitments in the Far East, Congress passed over President Hoover's veto a bill promising early independence to the Philippines, with a number of reservations attached. The island legislature rejected this enactment. Congress then, in the first month of the Roosevelt Administration, passed the more liberal McDuffie-Tydings Act (March 24, 1934). This gave the Filipinos full control over their islands, effective when a new constitution came into force in the fall of 1935, but pledged the United States to defend them until the transition period ended on December 31, 1944. They were to become fully independent on July 4, 1946. Under this law the Philippines soon became a self-governing Commonwealth, with their own President, Manuel Quezon.

Against this relationship of "responsibility without authority" many American experts protested. The legislation was generally selfish in motive, and not farsighted in terms. In approving it, Roosevelt expressed his belief that "where imperfections or inequalities exist," they would be corrected. Nicholas Roosevelt at once pointed out in *Foreign Affairs* (July, 1935), that a great risk was being taken. "Japan's long-range overseas policy seems for some time to have had the Dutch East Indies as its ultimate objective. The Philippines are in her path." And he added that the Oriental psychology was such that withdrawal from the islands, whether in ten years or at once, "will be interpreted in the Far East as final proof of the timidity of the United States and of its unwillingness to protect its own best interests." Fortunately, the Filipino leaders were fully awake to the Japanese threat, and President Quezon in 1935 asked President Roosevelt to let him have the services of the retiring Chief of Staff, General Douglas MacArthur. Going to Manila, MacArthur (with the aid of various American officers, among whom for a time was one named Dwight D. Eisenhower) acted first as military advisor to the Commonwealth Government, and then as Field Marshal commanding the Filipino army, striving to build up a force strong enough to hold off any invader until American help arrived.

CHAPTER VII

THE AMERICAN NEIGHBORS

WHILE the situation in Europe and the Far East was deteriorating under the impact of the world-wide depression, in one broad area American foreign relations steadily improved. Under President Coolidge the first steps toward a friendly understanding with Mexico proved a brilliant success, while under President Hoover the "Good Neighbor policy" with all Latin America (a phrase which Hoover invented) began to pay handsome dividends in confidence and amity. Meanwhile, it was a basic principle of American foreign policy to maintain the most cordial relations with Great Britain and other members of the British Commonwealth of Nations; and Canada became a closely linked partner of the United States.

The old Latin-American fear of northern domination, of the *Peligro Yanqui*, made it vitally important to instill more tact and altruism into American policy. As late as 1930 realistic students could assert that while Hispanic America had participated in the official machinery of Pan-American-icanism since James G. Blaine's day, the Latin nations placed no real faith in it. They often talked of revolt against its "dangers." Their wary publicists called the recurrent conferences (the sixth was held in Havana in 1928) "congresses of mice presided over by a cat"; they termed the central Washington office "the Ministry of Colonies"; and they declared Pan-Americanism a thin disguise for "North American imperialism." Latin-American suspicion of Yankee motives, feeding on memories of the annexation of half of Mexico's domain in 1848, the seizure of the Panama Canal route by Theodore Roosevelt, and "dollar diplomacy" under Taft, was also nourished by more recent grievances. After the First World War, conservative Americans had failed to comprehend the intensity of the movement for much-needed social and economic reforms in Mexico, Chile, and other republics. Those who had investments to the south failed to comprehend that foreign property interests were bound to suffer about as much as vested domestic interests in the violent overturns that took place.

The American policy of armed intervention to protect life and property in revolutionary areas, applied under Taft, Wilson, Harding, and Coolidge, created a natural exasperation. Sometimes this intervention in unruly little countries was prolonged, as in the control of Nicaragua from 1912 to 1932;

sometimes the financial receivership which accompanied it seemed illiberal, as in Haiti. The United States could be accused of maintaining as distinct a puppet government in Nicaragua as the one which the Japanese set up in Manchuria. It was a Conservative government, though a majority of the Nicaraguans were Liberals; and in return for American support, it gave Washington control over the bank, the railway, and the custom houses. Latin Americans well remembered how even the idealistic Wilson had sent troops into Haiti in 1915 and how an American Admiral had presently telegraphed the Navy Department: "Next Thursday . . . unless otherwise directed I will permit Congress to elect a President." They recalled an indiscreet boast of Franklin D. Roosevelt, when Assistant Secretary of the Navy, in 1920: "The facts are that I wrote Haiti's Constitution myself, and if I do say it, I think it is a pretty good constitution." They remembered how the Marines had gone into Santo Domingo. They knew that in 1927 the United States had more than 5,000 Marines and bluejackets active in Nicaragua to keep a rebel general from capturing the capital.

Economic relations between the United States and Latin America had meanwhile become highly complicated. The First World War gave the republic the place formerly held by Great Britain as chief supplier of capital to other parts of the Hemisphere. Latin-American bond issues were offered, aggregating $230,000,000 in 1921 and $224,000,000 in 1922. Along with this lending went entrepreneurial investment on a huge scale. The great industrial corporations of the United States formed affiliates, which spread from the Rio Grande to Cape Horn. Both American exports to and imports from Latin America climbed steeply until 1929, thereafter falling off more steeply still. The chief exports were such mass-production articles as automobiles, radios, talking machines, and films, with machinery of various kinds. The principal imports were the coffee and rubber of Brazil; the coffee and petroleum of Colombia; the tin, nitrates, and copper of Chile and Bolivia; the sugar of Cuba, and the bananas of Central America. The economies of the two parts of the Hemisphere were thus to a great extent complementary. Repeatedly, the value of the annual shipments to South America alone exceeded half a billion dollars. The United States was rich and in the period of the Coolidge-Hoover bull market, the era of "la dansa de los millones," it seemed even richer than it was; most of Latin America was very poor.

As business contacts multiplied, assiduous and somewhat artificial efforts were made to cultivate cultural relations as well. Geographically, a great part of South America lies nearer Europe than to the United States, and it was to Europe that the

Latin republics had always looked in letters, art, and philosophy. Those large elements which were of Indian origin (and Indian blood predominates in Mexico, Guatemala, Ecuador, Bolivia, and Peru, as Negro blood does in Haiti, and Negro and Indian in Brazil) cared little for any external influence. The population of Hispanic ancestry, however, counted Lisbon, Madrid, and Paris among their intellectual capitals as citizens of the United States counted London. On the one side lay nations largely Catholic, agrarian, impractical, and idealistic in outlook; on the other lay a nation largely Protestant, industrial, and while by no means lacking in idealism, given up to a cult of driving efficiency. The Latin Americans, as their frequent revolutions and dictatorships proved, had political beliefs differing essentially from those of the United States and Canada. The gulf seemed wide. But well-financed efforts were nevertheless made to exchange university teachers and students, arrange lectureships, establish English libraries in South America and Spanish libraries in the United States, foster the teaching of the two languages, and entertain delegations of Latin-American editors, politicians, and merchants. The Universities of Texas and California became notable centers of Latin-American studies, and not a few Latin-American classics were translated and published in the United States. In Washington the Pan-American Union, governed by a board representing all the American republics, encouraged closer intellectual as well as commercial relations.

It was essential for Americans to realize that Latin America had become mature and must be regarded in all its parts as an equal. The great dividing date between the old policy and the new in Washington's political treatment of Latin America was 1927, and the first figure to gain renown as an architect of a better order was the scholarly New York financier, Dwight W. Morrow. Circumstances made Mexico a test case in the internal struggle—so widespread in Latin America—between the old feudalism and the new reform spirit; they also made this partner in J. P. Morgan & Co., who happened to be one of the best-read and most liberal-spirited men of his time, the creator of a beneficent new attitude.

In 1911 a revolutionary movement of highly anti-capitalistic tendency had overthrown the dictatorship of Porfirio Diaz. One object of the revolution was to regain all the natural resources of Mexico for the nation. Americans had become large landholders in the northern states. In 1901 Edward L. Doheny and his associates had drilled the first oil well in Mexico, and American and British capital had developed a huge oil industry centering in Vera Cruz and Tabasco. By 1921 Mexico, with a total output of nearly two hundred million barrels, was the second largest oil-producing nation in the world. Article 27 of the new reform constitution of 1917, vesting the subsoil resources of Mexico in the Government, offended powerful foreign interests which feared that the principle might be made retroactive. It was aimed at greedy alien exploitation of petroleum and other minerals, just as a new agrarian program for breaking up the great estates was aimed largely at alien exploitation of the soil. These reforms presented so direct a threat to American oil, mining, and ranching interests, including those of William Randolph Hearst, that a vociferous demand for intervention arose. It gained support from many Catholics who were irritated by the anti-clerical policies of the new Mexican regime. First Wilson and then Harding had refuseed to recognize President Obregon until in 1923 the Mexican Government at the Bucareli conference tacitly agreed to validate American subsoil rights acquired before 1917. The next year President Plutarco E. Calles came into power. He showed a distinct tendency to give a retroactive interpretation to the Constitution of 1917 and to carry out land reforms in a way unjust to legitimate American interests.

The situation for a time became steadily more tense until it seemed highly dangerous. By the summer of 1927 the controversy had given rise to rumors of war, which a few took seriously. The principal dispute at the moment was over a new statute of 1925 requiring American owners of oil lands to exchange their titles for fifty-year leases. While most American holders accepted this law, corporations controlled by Edward L. Doheny, Harry F. Sinclair, the Mellons, and other powerful men, did not. The American Ambassador was James R. Sheffield, a conservative New York lawyer who was unsympathetic to the revolution and overzealous in trying to defend American rights. He had filled Secretary Kellogg with his own fears and prejudices. President Coolidge on April 25, 1927, declared that "persons and property of a citizen are a part of the domain of the nation even when abroad," which was extreme doctrine; while Secretary Kellogg in a public address conjured up the foolish apparition of a "Mexican-fostered Bolshevik hegemony intervening between the United States and the Panama Canal." This attempt to connect the Calles regime with Moscow gave great offense in Mexico, which grew more defiant than ever.

Then, happily, Sheffield resigned. Since juridical arguments could accomplish nothing, the time had obviously come for a new approach. In July the President asked his Amherst classmate Dwight Morrow, who had done useful financial work for the Cuban Government, to take the Embassy; and against the advice of his partners, Morrow accepted. The short, genial, intensely vital amateur of diplomacy was soon delighting all observers. Writes Harold Nicolson:

From the first moment of his arrival it became obvious even to the most nationalistic Mexican that Morrow had come to placate, to appreciate, and to please. His insatiable friendliness, his utter simplicity, the very exuberance of his good will, held them enthralled. He applauded their food, their climate, their agriculture, their hats, their ancient monuments, the bamboo cages in which they kept their tame parrots, their peasant industries, their patriotism, their volcanoes, even their finances. Here at last was a North American who neither patronized nor sneered.

In dealing with specific disputes, Morrow's record was a mixture of success and failure. He settled for the time the almost insoluble problem of American oil rights. The question, he told President Calles, was legal, not diplomatic, and the Mexican Supreme Court ought to rule upon it; if that body would follow precedents set in the Texas Oil Company cases, a satisfactory adjustment would be in sight. Calles startled the Ambassador by saying that such a decision could be expected in about two months. Indeed, within a fortnight the court declared the petroleum law of 1925 unconstitutional. Morrow then arranged a compromise which granted American oil interests permanent concessions in developed wells, and certain preferential rights in their undeveloped holdings. The question of rights to agricultural and ranch holdings Morrow put on a better footing, but did not finally settle. In the bitter quarrel between state and church he achieved a truce, which was a remarkable accomplishment; but he declared that the vital core of the controversy could not be reached except by long and slow effort. He found that the question of the defaulted Mexican debt also defied any early solution.

What he did memorably effect was a new and friendlier attitude between the two neighbors. His methods were later accurately described by his friend Sir Arthur Salter. In every negotiation, Morrow tried industriously, wrote Salter, to understand the real interests and the deepest preoccupations of all the parties. In this spirit, he was quick to reach a sympathetic personal understanding with Calles, whose statesmanlike qualities he appreciated. Two shrewd strokes were the bringing of Charles A. Lindbergh, just after his transatlantic flight, to Mexico City, where he received a tumultuous ovation, and the importation of the humorist Will Rogers for speeches and handshakes. Morrow's frankness, friendliness, and spontaneity were often unconventional—when Calles announced to the Mexican Congress in 1928 that institutions were more important than men and that he could not accept reelection, Morrow leaned from the diplomatic box with hearty handclaps; but as he liked the Mexican people, so they liked him.

A bright new page was meanwhile being written in Nicaragua. That little republic, about equal in area to New York State, was important to the United States not for its coffee, sugar, and bananas, but as neighbor of Panama and possible seat of another isthmian canal. Its internal history for a hundred years had been disorderly. In 1893 a corrupt intriguer, Jose Santos Zelaya, had begun a sixteen-year dictatorship. Forced out of power by a Conservative revolution in 1909, he gave way to a more orderly and honest regime. The Conservative leaders found the country bankrupt and the demands of foreign creditors far greater than the revenues. They turned to the State Department for counsel and aid, with the result that a plan of financial reform drafted by Thomas C. Dawson (1910) was slowly put into effect. In a whole series of operations affecting monetary reform, reorganization of the customs service, management of the national bank, and strengthening of the railroad system, Americans participated with official encouragement from Washington. When revolt threatened the Conservative Government in 1912, American Marines were sent to the country, which they helped to pacify. Thereafter a small guard of Marines remained at the legation in Managua. The United States inescapably exerted an influence in elections, assisting to keep the Conservatives in power for twenty years. Electoral procedure became the target of bitter criticism, and in 1922 Dr. H. W. Dodds wrote a fairer law for the country.

Undoubtedly the United States conferred great benefits upon Nicaragua; but the situation was so uncomfortable for both nations that in an effort to terminate it, Washington in 1925 withdrew the legation guard. At once a new revolutionary struggle broke out, and it seemed necessary next year to send back the Marines. For one reason, Great Britain and other countries hinted that if America did not protect foreigners as it had undertaken to do under the Roosevelt corollary of the Monroe Doctrine, they might have to intervene. For another reason, revolutionary Mexico was giving vigorous support to the Nicaraguan revolutionaries. Secretary Kellogg rather hastily recognized the Conservatives under Diaz, while Mexico recognized the Liberals under Sacasa. While America sent arms to one faction, Mexico sent them to the other. The war grew bloody and merciless. The oligarchic groups on both sides recruited their forces by impressing helpless peons; guerrilla operations ravaged the countrysides and drove workers from the fields; prisoners were summarily shot. The United States increased its detachments until early in 1927 it had more than 5,000 troops in Nicaragua, waging what critics of the Administration termed Coolidge's private war in behalf of investors.

In his embarrassment Coolidge turned to Henry L. Stimson, sending him in the spring of 1927 as special emissary to the war-torn land. Since resentment was rising in Latin America, the action came none too soon. Stimson tactfully conferred with leaders of all schools. He found that the conflict was hopelessly stalemated, that the great majority of Nicaraguans were utterly sick of it, and that most men on both sides would be glad to have it ended by American mediation and good offices, including supervision of a national election. Three weeks after Stimson landed a detailed settlement was drawn up. It provided that Diaz should continue to hold the Presidency until 1928, both sides meanwhile disarming, with a general amnesty for all rebels; and that in 1928 the regular national election should be held under American guarantees of a fair vote. A new constabulary, trained and initially led by American Marines, should preserve civil order. Stimson found that, as he put it, "trust begets trust"; once he had convinced the two parties that his mission was disinterested and his object the restoration of independence and peace, their leaders in general proved reasonable and cooperative. In the elections, supervised by General Frank R. McCoy, the Liberals won; and with Conservative acquiescence, José Maria Moncada was inaugurated President. Only a guerrilla leader named Sandino, commanding a small bandit force in almost impenetrable jungle, continued to disturb the peace, and in 1932 he finally surrendered.

"Thus the United States," writes Stimson, "at some expense and with considerable effort, succeeded in this one war in substituting ballots for bullets." When Hoover became President and Stimson his Secretary of State, they acted to withdraw the major part of the American forces. By September, 1929, they had reduced the Marines to 2,215, and they kept on reducing them, merely using a small number to train a new National Guard and keep the peace until it took control. The Presidential election of 1932 was again conducted under American supervision. Meanwhile, in the spring of 1931 Stimson warned American citizens that they could not expect protection in the areas threatened by Sandino, and he urged them to withdraw, if necessary, to the safe coastal towns. Upon the inauguration of Dr. Juan B. Sacasa, the Marines were withdrawn on January 2, 1933. Though they had been much assailed in the United States and throughout Latin America, actually the troops had performed a constructive work of disarmament and policing with efficiency and tact, and they left Nicaragua far more peaceful and industrious than when they came.

In other areas, too, the Hoover-Stimson policy achieved happy results. Immediately before his inauguration President-elect Hoover made a good-will circuit of the chief South American ports. At the same time J. Reuben Clark, Under-Secretary of State with Kellogg, was preparing a 230-page memorandum on the history of the Monroe Doctrine, which the State Department issued in 1930. Clark accurately stated the real limits of Monroe's state paper, making it clear that it did not sanction intervention, and thus paving the way to a repudiation of the Roosevelt corollary. The Doctrine, he wrote, stated a case of the United States as against the Old World, and not a case of the United States as against Latin America. "So far as Latin America is concerned, the Doctrine is now, and always has been, not an instrument of violence and oppression, but an unbought, freely bestowed, and wholly effective guarantee of their freedom, independence, and territorial integrity against the imperialistic designs of Europe."

This was a statement which the Caribbean and South American nations found reassuring. Taking full credit for it later, Hoover declared: "I had the old Theodore Roosevelt interpretation of the Monroe Doctrine revised from the concept of right to interference into a declaration of Western Hemisphere solidarity, of freedom from old world encroachment." While this revision did not recognize

the growing Latin-American desire to make the
Doctrine a matter of multinational concern, supported by all the nations on equal terms instead of
by the United States alone, and while it did not
assuage the resentful feeling of many people in
the southern republics that they did not need any
protector, it was excellent as far as it went. Neither
Hoover nor Stimson had any belief in the Roosevelt corollary. At one time it might have been
proper for the United States, since it denied any
European right to intervene, to accept a duty of
intervention itself when a Latin-American Government ceased to protect foreign lives and property;
if so, that time had passed. The rising nationalism
of Latin America, the growing world revolt against
all forms of semi-colonial control, and the bad results of too-hasty interference, had ushered in a
new era.

In line with this "deliberate pursuit of noninter-
ference," as Stimson called it, the United States
took steps to withdraw from Haiti. That country
was less well equipped than Nicaragua to paddle
its own canoe; still, the American occupation,
which had been provoked by violent disorders in
1915, was causing much discontent. While Marines
policed the little republic, American agencies furnished close financial supervision. The country was
practically a protectorate. A new chapter was
opened when on December 7, 1929, Hoover asked

Congress to authorize the appointment of an official commission to examine the situation and determine when and how American forces could best be withdrawn. Cameron Forbes headed this body, and William Allen White was an active member of it. As soon as the commission submitted an orderly plan for withdrawal, it was put into effect. A popularly elected government under Stenio Vincent was installed in 1930; measures were taken to rebuild the local government; and in 1931 American officials withdrew from the Departments of Agriculture, Public Works, and Sanitation. Financial controls were terminated, the National City Bank being persuaded to sell the National Bank of Haiti to the island authorities. Thus nearly every preparation was made for the complete withdrawal that took place under Hoover's successor.

Under Woodrow Wilson, a strong moral attitude, a desire to back "good" governments and discourage "bad" regimes, had strengthened the interventionist tendency. It was the conviction of Hoover and Stimson that the moralistic approach did more harm than good. They returned to the historic American policy of promptly recognizing *de facto* governments. This was less meddlesome, less aggressive, and less troublesome. They also adopted the practice of withholding arms and munitions from rebels. In March, 1929, a revolt broke out in Mexico. Relations with that republic, since

Morrow's work, were good; Congress had recommended an arms embargo policy by joint resolution in 1922, and the Administration promptly shut off arms from the insurrectionists. When the revolt failed, public opinion applauded its action. In 1930 a similar embargo was applied against revolutionary forces in Brazil. This time the rebels succeeded, and Stimson found himself exposed to embarrassing criticism. Cheerfully recognizing the new Brazilian Government, he shrugged off the attacks; it was not his business, he said, to take sides or to pick winners, but simply to give recognition and support to existing governments. An inter-American treaty of 1928 sanctioned this policy.

One of the most brilliant achievements of President Hoover in Latin-American relations was his settlement of the thorny Tacna-Arica dispute. This dated back to the early 1880's. Then, following the war of Chile, Peru, and Bolivia, it had been provided by treaty that Chile should hold these annexed provinces for ten years, when a plebiscite should determine their formal disposition. Unhappily, the nations concerned could never agree on the terms of the plebiscite. After much quarreling, they arranged in 1922 to submit the issue to arbitration by the President of the United States. Three years later Coolidge decided that an election should be held under a commission representing Chile,

Peru, and the United States. This plan broke down, however, when the American Chairman, General William Lassiter, voted with the Peruvian representative to halt the proceedings on the ground that the Chilean authorities were making a free vote impossible. Hoover on becoming President took up the matter, and at his instance Chile and Peru agreed in 1929 upon a division of the disputed territory. An ideal solution would have given landlocked Bolivia an outlet to the sea in this area; but at any rate this was a working solution.

In every way, Hoover and Stimson labored to satisfy legitimate Latin-American aspirations. In dealing with the dispute of Bolivia and Paraguay over the district called the Gran Chaco, for example, they showed anxiety to collaborate with the leading South American nations and the League; on both counts this pleased the southern continent. It was their rule to replace political Ambassadors and Ministers in Hispanic America by career men who knew something of the language and people. Hoover denounced dollar diplomacy as "cupidity encroaching upon the weakness of nations." He and Stimson refused to meddle in the internal affairs of Cuba despite the invitation given them by the bad political state of the island; they neither opposed the corrupt and tyrannical Government of President Machado nor gave any encouragement to it. The Presidents-elect of Mexico, Colombia, and

Brazil, visiting Washington, met a cordial reception. Gradually the Latin-American nations learned to respect American purposes; and they repaid Hoover and Stimson by adopting their doctrine of non-recognition of conquests made by force. When at the beginning of 1928 Hughes had headed a strong delegation to the Sixth Pan-American Conference, meeting in Havana, he had encountered deep suspicion, and the Americans had with difficulty blocked a non-intervention resolution aimed directly at them. But by 1930 the Good Neighbor policy was a reality on both sides.

Canadian relations, too, were kept on a high plane of amity. Secretary Stimson has written that cooperation with Great Britain was in many ways the touchstone of his policy, and this implied cooperation with the Dominion. In 1927 the Canadian Government established a Legation in Washington, appointing Vincent Massey as its first Minister, and the United States reciprocated by sending William Phillips as first resident Minister to Ottawa. Various friendly treaties and conventions were concluded in 1920–30. When in 1929 the Coast Guard sank a Canadian rum-running schooner, the *I'm Alone*, off the Louisiana shore, the ensuing controversy was submitted to arbitration. The sequel was an apology from the American Government, and the ultimate payment of slightly over $50,000 as compensation.

Both the Hoover Administration and the Canadian Government took a keen interest in the movement for cutting a deep waterway from the Great Lakes to the Atlantic through the St. Lawrence channel. A favorable report on this project was made by the International Joint Commission in 1921, and was supported by two reports by a joint engineering board in 1927 and 1932, and by two economic commissions, one American and one Canadian, in 1926 and 1928. With this weight of expert opinion behind the scheme, its advocates hoped for an early victory. A treaty for joint action was drawn up, which Secretary Stimson signed on July 18, 1932. Hoover hailed it as "another step forward in this the greatest internal improvement yet undertaken on this continent." Besides providing for constructions of different sections of the waterway, the treaty covered the use of water for hydroelectric power and the protection of water levels. Early in 1933, Hoover submitted the treaty to the Senate with a recommendation for approval, and a month later the Foreign Relations Committee gave the plan its qualified approbation. Meanwhile, however, opposition from Atlantic ports had arisen, and a long delay supervened.

As the international situation in Europe and the Orient grew darker after 1930, the fact that two great political aggregations, the Latin-American republics and the British Commonwealth of Nations, stood in a relation of staunch friendliness toward the United States was of incalculable comfort to the directors of American policy. Most Americans took this cordiality as a matter of course, but that fact did not lessen its importance.

CHAPTER VIII

THE BREAKDOWN OF DISARMAMENT

It was not economic problems and the Far East alone which held the attention of Europe and America in 1931–32; the broad question of disarmament also engaged the energies of statesmen. As the depression deepened, the burden of taxes for battleships and armies was felt more keenly. Above all, however, men felt that competition in armaments had been one of the main roots of the First World War, and believed that they must cut that taproot of a second conflict. If they did not, new weapons would be perfected, mobilization of nations would become more nearly total, and the awful destruction and mortality of 1914–18 would be surpassed by new holocausts. Winston Churchill had struck a prophetic note in 1925. "May there not be methods of using explosives incomparably more intense than anything heretofore discovered?" he wrote. "Might not a bomb no bigger than an orange be found to possess a secret power to destroy a whole block . . . ?" Could not explosives even of the older types, he added, be guided automatically in aircraft or aerial torpedoes, by radio without a human pilot, in relentless procession upon a hostile city, arsenal, or army encampment? To forestall such terrors, the nations must agree to limit or abolish armaments.

The Versailles Treaty had expressed the honorable intention of Wilson, Clemenceau, Lloyd George, and their associates to organize the world so that armed forces might be gradually reduced and eventually eliminated. But the task proved unexpectedly difficult. As we have noted, it fell into two unequal parts. The lesser problem was that of naval limitation; with the United States and Britain leading, the Washington Conference of 1922 and the London Conference of 1930 made encouraging progress toward the goal. Much more formidable was the task of general disarmament, binding all nations and embracing all types of weapons. The Covenant had laid this undertaking upon the League, which was to carry it out "taking account of the geographical situation and circumstances of each state." For ten years little was done. The movement made progress when liberal men like MacDonald, Stresemann, and Briand were in office, but faltered when conservatives like Baldwin and Poincaré took power. America and Russia were not members of the League, and their cooperation was indispensable.

The fundamental difficulty, in the eyes of French leaders, of Winston Churchill, and even of Secretary Stimson, was that heavy armaments were not so much a cause as a result of international insecurity, and that full political guarantees would have to precede disarmament. The French had what was considered the strongest army in the world. If the United States and the British Commonwealth would guarantee the safety of France, Gallic leaders would gladly reduce that army; if not, they would maintain it. Beginning in 1926 an international preparatory commission worked on the larger aspects of the disarmament problem. One of the thorniest questions it faced, in dealing with land armaments, was how to estimate the military strength of the nations. Should trained reserves be counted? France, Belgium, Italy, Czechoslovakia, and other countries which had conscription, and hence large reserves, said "No." The United States, Britain, and Germany, which had small professional forces and no reserves, said "Yes." This conflict of opinion produced a deadlock until 1928–29, when first Great Britain and then the United States gave way. They did so because they realized they could never obtain the cooperation of France in arms reduction on any other terms. It then became possible for the preparatory commission to complete its draft of a broad disarmament treaty in December, 1930.

The quarrels which attended the making of this draft offered a bad augury for the future. Just how *could* armaments be controlled? The Versailles Treaty had restricted the German navy by tonnage, or on a quantitative basis; but the Germans evaded the restriction by emphasizing qualitative factors. They built a pocket-battleship of 10,000 tons so efficient that in many respects it equaled far larger warships. Qualitative competition might undo any quantitative limit. Again, how should strength in small weapons (bombs, guns, airplanes) be kept under check? Such armaments could easily be concealed. When it was proposed to control them by limiting the national budgets for air, naval, and ground forces, the United States raised vigorous objections; its level of costs and pay was much higher than in other countries. It was then suggested that each nation's annual arms budget be limited in relation to its own previous budgets. This plan encountered less American criticism and was included in the draft treaty.

Still another topic of contention lay in the question of inspection. In Germany an interallied commission, charged with enforcing the disarmament provisions of the peace treaty, had conducted investigations which the French declared did not go far enough, and which the Germans maintained went too far. When the French declared that it would be useless to ratify a general disarmament

treaty unless some international agency of inspection was created, Americans protested. For one reason, they could not permit any League agency to enforce the treaty. For another, they asserted that treaties properly rested upon the good faith of nations, and that it would be intolerable to have international officials snooping about every navy yard, ordnance plant, and munitions factory. On this point a compromise was finally worked out by a subcommittee. With an American member concurring, it recommended that each nation be required to supply full information on its armaments, that a permanent commission be set up at Geneva to scrutinize the reports, and that this body report regularly to the world. The draft treaty, in response to American demands, also contained an escape clause not unlike that in the London Naval Treaty. Under its terms, any country which faced a sudden threat to its safety might suspend the limitations on its armaments until the peril passed; but it must explain its reasons to the world, and must resume its treaty obligations as soon as possible.

Early in 1931 the draft treaty was sent to all the powers, and a plenary World Disarmament Conference was called to sit at Geneva in February, 1932. Most leaders the world over expected little from this gathering. Yet a few believed that the need for relief from the crushing burden of military preparation was so exigent, and the folly of arms

competition so obvious, that a brilliant success might be attained. Innumerable liberal people hoped that, once representatives of all the nations met in a single room and faced realities, they might agree in a smashing attack on selfishness and fear. Secretary Stimson was among the doubters. He warned the British Ambassador at the beginning of 1931 that no great result could be reached unless the three nations chiefly interested in reducing armies, France, Germany, and Italy, should first "get together and grapple with the fundamental questions which lie at the bottom of such disarmament." That is, they should do what MacDonald and Hoover had done on the Rapidan log before the London Naval Conference. But 1931 passed without any action to lay the foundations for success.

The United States sent to Geneva a delegation headed by Hugh Gibson, and including Norman H. Davis, Senator Claude A. Swanson, and President Mary Woolley of Mount Holyoke College. Secretary Stimson himself, when the Conference fell into the doldrums, went to Europe to talk to national leaders. Failure, however, could not be averted. What happened, in brief, was that the powers argued at Geneva from February to July, 1932, without result; adjourned while international negotiations reexplored the ground; met again in February, 1933, just after Hitler had risen to power,

and promptly found themselves deadlocked once more; were presented first with a new British plan and then with a new American plan offered in the hope of breaking the impasse; and after continued wrangling, adjourned in the summer of 1933, with nothing whatever accomplished. No debacle could have been more complete.

The fundamental difficulty was that France and her allies of the Little Entente insisted that political arrangements for security should take precedence over disarmament measures; while the better protected nations, notably the United States and Britain, argued that if disarmament measures were honestly carried through, the improved atmosphere would make political arrangements for security far easier. Each side could defend its position with logical arguments. To the Anglo-Saxon mind, the French evinced a deplorable combination of vindictiveness and panic in facing Germany; if they would but show generosity of spirit, the Germans would show generosity in return. The French emphasis on security involved a relentless maintenance of every clause of the Versailles Treaty. This was absurd; Laval admitted to Stimson that parts of Versailles were wrong and harmful, though he added that revision was politically impossible. To most American and British leaders, French suspicion and harshness were bound in time to create a Germany bent on revenge. The French looked at matters

from an entirely different standpoint. They believed that as Germany had waged a war of aggression in 1870 and another in 1914, so she would wage a third if opportunity offered. They suspected that Germany was already secretly rearming. Until they had definite guarantees from a collective security system stronger than the League, the French believed that retention of their powerful army was a matter of life or death.

This disagreement made success at Geneva impossible. Great Britain would and at Locarno did pledge herself to defend the boundaries of France and Belgium, but she would not pledge men and treasure to maintain eastern European boundaries. The United States would make no political commitments whatever for France. Laval had raised the question of a very limited pledge in the fall of 1931. He asked Stimson for an agreement binding the United States to consult with France if a breach of the Briand-Kellogg Pact were threatened. President Hoover at once declared this a political impossibility.

The American delegates at Geneva tried to find a way through the deadlock by a plan for removing fear of aggression. They suggested that security for all would be attained if the great aggressive weapons, including tanks, heavy mobile artillery, and gases, were forbidden. When committees were appointed to determine just what types of armament

were aggressive, however, they ran into insuperable obstacles. Every nation regarded its favorite weapons as defensive and those of its neighbors as offensive. The French declared that battleships and heavy cruisers were implements of aggressive warfare, while submarines were defensive types; the British and Americans asserted that submarines were offensive weapons, and battleships were merely defensive. The obstacles remained as great as ever. But President Hoover regarded the American principle as sound, and suddenly intervened with a new application.

His plan was bold, ingenious, and at first glance highly promising. It called for a flat reduction of one-third in the tonnage of battleships; for the abolition of bombing planes and prohibition of bombing; and for the interdiction of tanks, big mobile ordnance, and chemical warfare. At the same time a sharp cut was to be made in all land forces above the level required to maintain order at home. This police force was to be based on a coefficient reflecting the ratio of the existing German army to the German population (one soldier to 650 people); additional troops were to be allowed for overseas possessions; but all armies above these levels were to be diminished by one-third. Hoover deserved great credit for so trenchant a scheme, which created a world-wide sensation. However, instant objections developed. France and the Little Entente

were aghast. They saw that the army-ratio plan
would give a great advantage to nations with large
and fast-growing populations; to Russia, Germany,
Italy, and Japan. These were the nations which
wished to upset the post-war settlement. When
Moscow, Berlin, and Rome eagerly applauded the
plan, the French found all their fears confirmed.
The Japanese and British objected to naval cuts,
while Britain also wished to retain small tanks.

A hasty effort was made to revise the Hoover
plan to make it more acceptable to the Allies and
less tempting to Germany and Russia. After a
month of secret negotiations, a modified version
was presented. Meeting little favor, it was jetti-
soned, even the American delegation voting against
some of its features. When the Conference adjourned in July, 1932, it had become clear that the
French were right; that armaments could not be
effectively reduced until the underlying political
tensions were dissolved. This had become more
difficult than ever. The Germans declared that they
would not reenter the Conference until their demand for equality of treatment was met—a demand
which made the French feel more insecure than
ever. With much labor, including not a little American assistance, a formula was found which satisfied the German claim in principle, and the second session of the Conference began in February,
1933.

In this session Hitler's shadow fell like a gloomy cloud across all the debates. Men had watched with grave misgiving the recent events in Germany; the discussions were accompanied by still graver occurrences. Delegates read of the firing of the Reichstag building on February 27, the organization of a frenzied Nazi electoral canvass by Dr. Joseph Goebbels, the winning of 281 Reichstag seats by Hitler as against 118 for the next largest party, and the grant on March 24 of complete emergency powers to Hitler for the next four years. Thus suddenly did a sinister dictatorship emerge in Germany! It was a revolution of the most dangerous character. More than that, storm signals were flying in other parts of the globe. While Mussolini was already flirting with expansionist schemes, Tokyo was showing its continued contempt for the League, and some fifty thousand of its troops were soon invading China proper through the province of Jehol. It is not strange that the delegates at Geneva labored under a sense of bleak discouragement. The end of February found the Conference again deadlocked. By that date the Hoover Administration was ending, and the United States lay waterlogged in the trough of the depression.

Two statesmen of the English-speaking nations had made European tours in 1932: Henry L. Stimson and Winston Churchill, later to be closely associated in directing the mightiest war effort in his-

tory. Both were farsighted men. Churchill was already deeply alarmed over the secret rearming of Germany. He believed that behind the democratic façade of the Weimar Constitution the real government of the Reich had for some time lain in the General Staff; he knew that the army chieftains were ready to contract an alliance with the Nazis. He was aware that with the aid of commercial and sports aviation a well-trained German air force had come into existence, that submarines were being illicitly built, and that under the leadership of Walther Rathenau, German war industries had been reconstructed. American and British loans had facilitated the rebuilding of factories which might speedily be converted to war uses. Working on his biography of Marlborough, Churchill visited old battlefields in Germany. He found a stir of martial activity and sensed a "Hitler atmosphere." Returning to Britain, he tried to awaken that country to the situation.

Churchill was convinced that in these locust years the British Government was showing almost incredible unwisdom, and the French Government almost incredible weakness. The pacifism of MacDonald, the preoccupation of Baldwin and Sir John Simon with business as usual, the shortsightedness of Briand and Laval, allowed the world situation constantly to worsen. Nor in his opinion could the United States escape severe censure. Absorbed in its

own economic affairs, it imagined that it could safely stand aloof from the troubles of other lands. Shrewd American diplomatists, publicists, and military men held another opinion, but their exhortations produced no effect upon what Churchill called "the improvident aloofness of American foreign policy." Had the United States exercised a due influence, it might have stimulated the leaders of France and Britain into action. Had it given full support to the League, participating in its political as well as humanitarian work, that battered but still potent instrument of international liberalism might have met the challenges to peace. But, as Churchill wrote later, the American nation simply watched and waited until they too in due time, found themselves in mortal peril.

The conclusions of Secretary Stimson were not dissimilar. He told Chancellor Bruening in Geneva on April 17, 1932, that the predicament of the world resembled the unfolding of a Greek tragedy, in which participants saw clearly the fatal march of events, but were helpless to avert the grim denouement. Events at Geneva bore him out. It was not learned until later that Ramsay MacDonald, Stimson, Norman H. Davis, and Bruening, conferring in April, devised a plan for heading off the Nazi movement in Germany. That movement fed upon the supposed humiliations of Germany; if the powers granted equality in armaments to the Reich,

the Weimar Constitution Government might be saved. Norman H. Davis, then Ambassador-at-Large, telephoned Premier Tardieu of France, begging him to come to Geneva. Unfortunately, Tardieu, for reasons good or bad, refused. That opportunity to bolster the Bruening Government, like the opportunity to help it by a timely remission of reparations, was lost. The fact was, as Stimson remarks in his memoirs, that by 1932 all the major powers were entrenched in self-righteous attitudes; all were cultivating highly emotional states of mind; and in all of them leaders were afraid of their electorates. Laval and Tardieu found any reasonable approach to Germany a "political impossibility"; Hoover found even a pledge to consult with France in time of trouble a "political impossibility."

As Europe's heritage of old enmities and fears was far greater than America's, so European blunders far exceeded in magnitude any made by the United States. As time passed, however, it became evident to all but the blindest that America's era of isolationism was one of the least creditable chapters in the history of her foreign relations. Some of the unhappier results of American policy were noted at the time by such Republican leaders as George Wickersham, Nicholas Murray Butler, and Elihu Root. Talking to Stimson, Root at the end of 1930 summed up some of the counts in a tenable indictment which other nations might bring against

the United States. One was that America, having
made a great deal of money out of the World War,
had then insisted on a rigid collection of debts from
impoverished Europe. Another was that, although
the United States had designed the League of Nations and urged it on the world as a means of pre-
serving peace, it had refused to join it. A third was
that America had treated the World Court in the
same way; it had largely created that valuable institution, and then had rejected it. The fourth count
was that the United States insisted upon retaining
the principle of neutrality; it thus left itself free in
the event of any new war to make money out of it
by selling munitions, and also left itself free to
burke any embargo which other peace-loving
nations might lay down against an aggressor.
Stimson, while regarding the first count as
overstated, believed that the other three were
unanswerable.

As the Hoover Administration ended and the
Roosevelt Administration began, the great test of
the world's ability to preserve peace was still to
come. Much ground had been lost; could it be re-
gained? France still seemed strong; Italy was still
in general committed to peace, and distrustful of
Hitler; the United States had a new leadership. If
the tragedy of 1932 in Europe was, as Stimson believed, a tragedy of the timidity of statemanship,
could not bolder statesmen be found? In the State
Department, the international-minded Stimson

now gave way to international-minded Cordell Hull. Immediately after the appointment was announced the two men began to confer on problems of foreign policy. On every important topic they found themselves in agreement; neither in Europe nor in the Far East would there be any marked reversal of attitude. But the last word in foreign relations is always uttered by the President; the important change was not from Stimson to Hull, but from Herbert Hoover to Franklin D. Roosevelt.

Viewed as a whole, the history of American foreign policy in this period seemed largely a retreat from world responsibilities. Actually, this was not true. A precipitate retreat had been attempted, but the nation was finding that it could not evade its due part in global affairs. The treaties resulting from the Washington Conference, the Kellogg-Briand Peace Pact, and the Hoover-Stimson Doctrine in fact went far toward revolutionizing the old American doctrines of international law. They destroyed the old-time conceptions which required a neutral state to treat belligerents alike even if one was a flagrant aggressor and the other totally innocent; and in doing so they laid a foundation for great future changes in American policy—changes leading directly to the Lend-Lease Act and to the Nuremberg Trial of Nazi war criminals. The United States could not remove itself from a key position in international affairs.

BIBLIOGRAPHICAL NOTE

THE volumes of *Foreign Affairs*, published somewhat irregularly by the Department of State, furnish what materials can properly be laid before the world on American external relations. They are supplemented by various collections of papers, of which the annual *Documents on International Affairs*, edited beginning 1928 for the Royal Institute of International Affairs by J. W. Wheeler-Bennett and Stephen Heald, are the most comprehensive. Much valuable source material is to be found in the monthly *International Conciliation* of the Carnegie Endowment for International Peace, together with articles of importance. Among periodicals the quarterly *Foreign Affairs* is indispensable, while files of *Current History* (ending 1936), the bi-monthly *International Affairs* (published by the Royal Institute), the *Manchester Guardian Weekly*, the semi-monthly *Foreign Policy Reports* prepared by the Foreign Policy Association, and the League of Nations *Official Journal*, are all of great value. Competent annual summaries of American foreign relations are to be found in the *American Year Book* and the *New International Year Book*.

A number of useful general surveys of the period have been written, usually from a world point of view. They include G. M. Gathorne-Hardy's highly compressed *Short History of International Affairs. 1920–1938* (1938); Dwight E. Lee's *Ten Year's: the World on the Way to War. 1930–1940* (1942); F. H. Soward's *Twenty-five Troubled Years, 1918–1943* (1944); Alfred Cobban's *The Crisis of Civilization* (1941); Arnold Wolfers, *Britain and France between Two Wars*; and C. S. Haines and Ross J. S. Hoffman, *The Origins and Background of the Second World War* (1947). Much more detailed are the annual one-volume surveys of *The United States in World Affairs* published year by year since 1931 by the Council on Foreign Relations. The authors of the volumes on the 1930's include Walter Lippmann, William O. Scroggs, and Whitney M. Shepardson. Histories of a somewhat more general nature, dealing with much besides international relations, are Stephen King-Hall, *Our Own Times, 1913–1934* (2 vols., 1935), Frederick L. Schumann, *Night over Europe* (1941), and Walter Millis, *Why Europe Fights* (1940).

Various specialized treatments have been given to the interrelationship between economics and international relations. One of the best general treatises is H. W. Arndt's *The Economic Lessons of the 1930's* (1944), a searching report based on group discussions held by the Royal Institute of International Affairs. Lionel Robbins in *The Economic Causes of War* (1939) finds that unrestrained national sovereignty in economic matters is one of the roots of conflict and argues that it must be limited. Antonín Basch in *A Price for Peace* (1945) examines some of the tremendous economic problems that pre-war Europe found insoluble. Two incisive books which invade the field of theory are Peter Drucker's *End of Economic Man*

(1939) and Herbert Feis's *Changing Pattern of International Economic Affairs* (1940). Both economic and political strands are treated by Allan Nevins and Louis M. Hacker, eds., *The United States and Its Place in World Affairs* (1943). J. P. Day's *Introduction to World Economic History since the Great War* (1939) is a compact summary. J. W. Angell's *The Recovery of Germany* (1929) deals with one key area, and Herbert Heaton's *The British Way to Recovery* (1934) with another.

Among books on the League, Lord Robert Cecil's *A Great Experiment* (1941) and Sir Alfred Zimmern's *The League of Nations and the Rule of Law* (1936) are specially enlightening. The best book on France is D. W. Brogan's *France under the Republic. 1870–1939* (1939); while Stephen H. Robert's *The House That Hitler Built* (1937), Louis Fischer's *The Soviets in World Affairs* (1930), Max Beloff's *The Foreign Policy of Soviet Russia, 1929–1936* (1947), and Herman Finer's *Mussolini's Italy* (1935) are all careful and scholarly. Raymond L. Buell has written on *Poland: Key to Europe* (1939), and E. Wiskemann on *Czechs and Germans* (1938). Hitler's *Mein Kampf* (Eng. tr., 1939) is of course indispensable to an understanding of the time. Vatican policy is ably covered by C. M. Cianfarra's *The Vatican and the War* (1944). The downfall of the Third French Republic is treated with mordant pen by André Geraud ("Pertinax") in *The Gravediggers of France* (1944), and the sequel in Leon Marchal's *Vichy: Two Years of Deception* (1944). For the small states of eastern Europe, see Antonín Basch, *The Danube Basin and the German Economic Sphere* (1943).

A flock of volumes of personal memoirs has illuminated the period under review. The *Memoirs* of Cordell Hull and those of Henry L. Stimson (both 1948) are of outstanding value. Among the other striking books are Stimson's *American Policy in Nicaragua* (1927) and *The Far Eastern Crisis* (1931); *Ambassador Dodd's Diary, 1933–38* (1941), a hostile picture of Berlin under Hitler; Sir Nevile Henderson's *Failure of a Mission* (1940), by the last English Ambassador to the Reich; Joseph C. Grew's *Ten Years in Japan* (1944), in diary form and hence somewhat undigested; Hugh R. Wilson's *Diplomat between Wars* (1941); *Behind the Japanese Mask*, by Sir Robert Craigie (1945); J. Alvarez del Vayo's *Freedom's Battle* (1940), on the Spanish revolution; *Mission to Moscow* by Joseph E. Davies (1941), which is a mixture of diary and confidential dispatches; *Wartime Mission in Spain*, by Carlton J. H. Hayes (1945); Sumner Welles's revealing *Time for Decision* (1944); and James F. Byrnes's still more revealing volume, *Speaking Frankly* (1947). Winston Churchill's speeches have been collected in three volumes, *The End of the Beginning*, *Onwards to Victory*, and *The Dawn of Liberation* (1943–45).

On Latin-American relations an interesting but journalistic general introduction is furnished by John Gunther's *Inside Latin America* (1941), the record of a rapid tour. More thorough treatments are provided in G. T. Whitaker, *Americas to the South* (1940), and W. L. Schurz's *Latin America* (1941). A good popular treatment of Latin-American history may be found in L. D. Baldwin's *The Story of the Americas* (1943), and an admirable study of the attitudes taken by

Washington in Samuel Flagg Bemis's *The Latin American Policy of the United States* (1943).

Far Eastern affairs for these years are the subject of a large library of volumes. Among the most important are A. Morgan Young's *Imperial Japan. 1926–1938* (1938) written by the editor of the *Japan Chronicle*; Owen Lattimore's *Solution in Asia* (1945), which dissects the dead body of Occidental imperialism; T. A. Bisson's *Japan in China* (1938); H. F. McNair's *China in Revolution* (1931); and Nathaniel Peffer's *Basis for Peace in the Far East* (1942). It need hardly be said that H. L. Stimson's *The Far Eastern Crisis* (1936) is invaluable for the subject it treats. A. W. Griswold has written in thorough and scholarly fashion an account of *The Far Eastern Policy of the United States* (1938).

In conclusion, it may be noted that the two best general treatments of American foreign policy from beginning to end are Samuel Flagg Bemis's *The Diplomatic History of the United States* (1936 and later editions), and Thomas A. Bailey's *A Diplomatic History of the American People* (1940 and later editions), both kept carefully down to recent date. D. F. Fleming has covered the subject of *The United States and World Organization. 1920–1933* (1938) in admirable fashion. Serviceable biographies of figures important in foreign affairs are available in David Bryn-Jones, *Frank B. Kellogg* (1937), Harold Nicolson, *Dwight Morrow* (1935), and Claudius O. Johnson, *Borah of Idaho* (1936), while William Starr Myers has compiled a useful volume, *The Foreign Policies of Herbert Hoover* (1940).

INDEX

AAA, 77

Abbott, Grace, 56

Adams, John, 23

Adee, Alvah A., 63

Agriculture, U. S., and tariffs, 141

Aircraft carriers, U. S., 131

Alaska, 18, 25

Alverstone, Lord, 25

Anglo-Japanese alliance, 107

Anschluss, 148 ff.; European reaction, 149 f.

Arbitration, in international disputes, 11 f.; and the League of Nations, 30; Hague Tribunal, 51

Armament, *see* Disarmament

Austria, economic distress, 147 f.; Kredit-Anstalt, 147 f., 150 f.; *Anschluss*, 148 ff.

Baker, Newton D., 191

Baldwin, Stanley, 85, 179, 233

Baldwin-Mellon war-debts agreement, 85 f.

Balfour, Arthur, 103, 105

Bank failures, 158 f.

Bank for International Settlements, 151 f., 155, 164

Bankhead Act, 77

Benes, Eduard, *re Anschluss*, 149 f.

Bennett, Richard B., 144

Beresford, Charles, Lord, 24

Big business, 67

Blaine, James G., 11

Bliss, Tasker H., 32

Bolivia, Tacna-Arica dispute, 217 f.; Gran Chaco dispute, 218

Bombs, in warfare, 222 f.

Borah, William E., 33, 100, 121; and naval reduction, 100 f.

Brazil, revolution of 1930, 217

Briand, Aristide, 105, 118, 125, 180, 185; quoted *re* outlawry of war, 122

British Commonwealth, 180; attitude toward the League, 99; *re* Anglo-Japanese alliance, 102; Ottowa Imperial Conference (1932), 143 f.

Bruening, Heinrich, 148, 152, 163, 180, 234

Bryan, William Jennings, 37; *re* "cooling-off" plan in international disputes, 95

Bucareli Conference (1923), 206

Butler, Nicholas Murray, 122, 235

California, University of, 204

Calles, Plutarco E., 206, 209

Canada, 18; and the U. S., 23, 219 ff.; disarmament policy, 98; *see also* British Commonwealth

Canadian-Alaskan boundary, 25

Castle, William R., 136

Cecil, Robert, Lord, 60 f., 178

Central America, "dollar diplomacy," 21

Chamberlain, Austen, 114, 118, 125

Chamberlain, J. P., 122

Chang Tso-lin, 174

Chiang Kai-shek, rise of, 172 f.; vs. the Communists, 197

Child, Richard Washburn, 63

Chile, Tacna-Arica dispute, 217 f.

China, Japan's Twenty-One Demands, 101; Nine-Power Treaty provisions *re*, 108 f.; chaotic situation in, 172 f.; Japanese investment in, 177; resistance to Japan, 177 f.; traditional U. S. friendliness toward, 188 f.; appeal to the League, 190; rise of Communism, 196 f.; Japanese invasion of Jehol, 232; *see also* Manchuria; Open Door policy

Chinchow, 178

Churchill, Winston, *re* explosives as weapons, 222 f.; European tour (1932), 232 f.

Clark, J. Reuben, 214

Clayton-Bulwer Treaty, 25

Clemenceau, Georges, *re* the League, 30

Cleveland, Grover, 18; extension of the Monroe Doctrine, 9

Collective security, 46, 58, 98

Communism, rise, in China, 196 f.

Coolidge, Calvin, *re* the League, 55; speech *re* the World Court, 115; and the treaty denouncing war, 124; doctrine *re* U. S. citizens abroad, 207

Cotton, Joseph P., 136

Council on Foreign Relations, 4

Cox, James M., 37

Cuba, 218

Currency hoarding, 158 f.

Curtius, Julius, 152

Customs Union (*Anschluss*), 148 ff.

Davis, Norman H., 227, 234 f.

Dawes, Charles G., 88, 128, 186

Dawes Plan, 89 ff.

Dawson, Thomas G., 210

Dearing, Fred M., 63

Declaration of Paris (1856), 13

Democracy, U. S. traditional support of, 5 ff., 46; in Japan, 175

Democratic party, platform (1920), 37

Depression of the 1930's, 137 ff.; effect on U. S. foreign policy, 139 ff.; bank failures, 158 f.; world-wide effects of, 158 ff.

Dewey, John, 121

Diaz, Porfirio, 205, 211

Dies, Martin, 161

Disarmament, 96 ff., 127 ff.; the League conventions *re*, 56 f.; breakdown of, 222 ff.; World Disarmament Conference, 223, 226 ff.; problem of land armaments, 224; difficulties of enforcement, 225 f.; draft treaty, 226 f.; European arguments *re*, 228 f.; aggressive vs. defensive arms, 230; Hoover's proposal, 230 f.; *see also* Naval limitation

Dodds, H. N., 211

Doheny, Edward L., 205

"Dollar diplomacy," 20 f.

Drummond, Sir Eric, 50

Economic nationalism, 65 ff., 140, 145 f.

Economic sanctions, 98, 183, 185 f., 191, 194

Economic warfare, effects of, 167 f.

Europe, pre-Wold War I, 27 f.; losses in World War I, 36; economic problems after World War I, 65 ff.; effect of high U. S. tariffs, 73; joint economic action in the early 1930's, 144 f.; *see also* Western powers

Extraterritoriality, 108 f.

Fall, Albert B., 42 f.

Far East, attitude toward Manchuria, 180

Far Eastern Conference (1921), 103 ff.

Federal Reserve System, 151

Feis, Herbert, 143

Fletcher, Henry P., 62

Forbes, Cameron, 216

Fordney-McCumber Act (1922), 72 ff.

Foreign loans, U. S., 74 ff., 138

Foreign Policy Association, 4

Foreign service, reorganization, 64

Four-Power Treaty, 107 f.

France, attitude toward war debts and reparations, 83 ff., 154 f., 162 f.; secret agreement with Britain on naval limitation, 127 f.; re naval limitation, 129; re Austrian *Anschluss,* 150 f.; relations with Germany, 150 f., 235; attitude toward Japan, 185; re disarmament, 228

Germany, reparations vs. war debts, 86 ff., 163; Locarno agreements re, 119; rise of Hitler, 148 ff.; *Anschluss,* 148 ff.; economic crisis, 150 ff.; elections (1933), 163 f.; French suspicion of, 228 f.; reaction to army-ratio plan, 230; secret rearming of, 233; *see also* Reparations

Gibson, Hugh, 227

Gilbert, Seymour Parker, 91, 153

Glass, Carter, 37

Goebbels, Joseph, 232

Gold standard, dropping of, 156 ff.

Good Neighbor policy, 200 ff.

Gran Chaco, 132, 218

Grant, Ulysses S., 18

Great Britain, sea power, 23; relations with the U. S., 23 ff.; war-debts policy, 83 ff.; Anglo-Japanese alliance (1902), 102; secret agreement with France *re* naval limitation, 127 f.; free trade policy, 145 f.; Seven-Power Conference, 155 ff.; effects of the economic crisis,

156 ff.; and the disarmament controversy, 228 ff.; early attitude toward Nazi Germany, 233; *see also* British Commonwealth

Grew, Joseph C., 62 f.

Guam, 101

Haiti, 22, 202; U. S. intervention, 215 f.

Hamaguchi, Yuko, 174, 176

Hanihara, *re* U. S. immigration law, 81, 105

Harding, Warren G., *re* the League, 39 f, 44, 55; characteristics, 40; close associates, 43

Harrison, George, 153

Harvey, George, 63; *re* U. S. foreign policy, 1

Hawaii, 18

Hay, John, 14; Open Door policy, 102

Hearst, William Randolph, 19, 206

Herrick, Myron T., 63

Herriot, Edouard, 164

Hindenburg, Paul von, 163; appeal to Hoover, 153

Hippisley, Arthur E., 24

Hitler, Adolf, 148 ff., 163, 232

Hoover, Herbert, World War library at Stanford, 4; *re* the League, 117; naval reduction, 128 f.; conference with Mac-Donald, 128 f.; background of experience, 135; administration, 136 f., 169, 179 f.; and the depression, 139 ff.; *re* Germany in the economic crisis, 152 f.; moratorium on war debts, 153 ff.; *re* foreign causes of U. S. depression, 160; war debts and reparations, 162 f.; *re* economic warfare, 167 f.; *re* the Manchurian crisis, 182 f.; Latin-American policy, 210 ff.; settlement of Tacna-Arica dispute, 217 f.; *re* the

St. Lawrence River waterway, 220; disarmament proposal, 230 f.

House, E. M., 32, 34

Hull, Cordell, 237

Hughes, Charles Evans, 42; policy *re* the League, 49 ff.; quoted, 62; as Secretary of State, 63; efforts *re* immigration law, 81; and reparations, 89 f.; address at the Far Eastern Conference (1921), 105 f.

Hymans, Paul, 49

I'm Alone (rum runner), 219

Immigration, 146; restrictive legislation, 78 ff.

Industry, U. S., boom of the 1920's, 74 ff.; in 1930, 138

International disputes, "cooling-off" treaties, 95 f.; Geneva Protocol, 117; *see also* Arbitration

International Economic Conference, 56

International relations, organization for the study of, 4; economic interdependence, 45

International trade, 68 ff., 138 f.; reaction to U. S. tariff acts, 142 ff.

Intervention, policy of, 18, 22, 201 f., 210 ff., 215 ff.

Irish Free State, 103

Isolationism, 6 f., 31 f.; and the League, 31, 34, 40; vs. the World Court, 113 f.; slogans, 162; results of, 235

Italy, resentment over U. S. immigration law, 82; war debts, 84; reaction to army-ratio plan, 231

Japan, post-World War I, 70; resentment over U. S. immigration law, 80 ff.; Twenty-One Demands on China, 101; Anglo-Japanese alliance (1902), 102; territorial expansion, 101 ff., 170; and the Nine-Power Treaty, 109 ff.; manhood suffrage law, 171; militarists vs. liberals, 170 f., 174 f.; economic distress, 174 f.; population increase, 175; Western powers and, 179 ff., 194 f.; world reaction to aggression in Manchuria, 179 f.; world opinion *re*, 192 f.; dependence on foreign trade, 183; triumph of the militarists, 195 f.; *see also* Manchuria

Jefferson, Thomas, 7; Embargo of 1807, 12

Johnson, Hiram, 33, 161

Jones Act of 1916, 20

Jusserand, Jean Jules, 105

Kato, Tomosaburo, 105

Kellogg, Frank B., 123 ff.; *re* Russian influence in Mexico, 207

Kellogg-Briand Pact, 117 ff., 181, 191, 229; effect, 126 f.

Keynes, John Maynard, 65, 166 f.

Knox, Frank, 73; *re* the Panama Canal, 21

Knox, Philander C., 67

Koo, Wellington, 105

Kredit-Anstalt, 147 f., 150 f.

Kuomintang, 173, 176

Lansing, Robert, 32

Lassiter, William, 218

Latin America, 133; and the U. S., 21 ff., 200 ff. (*see also* Monroe Doctrine); depression fears, 146 f.; imports and exports, 203; cultural relations with the U. S., 204; peoples of, 204

Lausanne Conference (1932), 16 ff.; reparations settlement, 164 f.

Laval, Pierre, conversations with Hoover, 159, 180

League of Nations, 28 ff.; member-states, 30 f., 48 f., 53; U. S. attitude toward, 30 ff., 99 f., 115 ff.; Covenant, Article X, 33, 98; early sessions, 48 ff.; organizations, 50 f.; settlement of disputes, 53 f.; activities, 54 f.; Opinion Committee, 51; effect of U. S. non-participation, 57 ff.; actual character of, 60; and the disarmament problem, 98 ff., 223; Geneva Protocol for the Pacific Settlement of International Disputes, 117; Preparatory Commission on Disarmament, 127, 132; *re* Austrian *Anschluss*, 150; and Manchuria, 178 ff.; appeal to Japan, 191 f.
Levinson, S. O., 121
Lincoln, Abraham, 6
Lindbergh, Charles A., 209
Lindley, Sir Francis, 185
Litvinov, Max, *re* war, 45; proposals *re* disarmament, 127
Lloyd George, David, *re* disarmament, 98; *re* Stimson, 186
Locarno agreements, 117 f., 229
Lodge, Henry Cabot, 105
Lowell, Abbott Lawrence, 191
Lytton Commission on Manchuria, 187 ff.; report adopted, 193 f.

MacArthur, Douglas, service in the Philippines, 199
McCoy, Frank R., 187, 212
MacDonald, Ramsay, 152, 233, 234; conference with Hoover, 128 f.; coalition ministry, 157 f.
McDuffie-Tydings Act (1934), 198
Machado, Gerardo, 218
McKinley, William, administration, 20
McKinley Tariff Act (1890), 142
Mahan, A. T., quoted, 19
Macmillan, Lord, report on the economic crisis, 157

Manchukuo, 192
Manchuria, Japanese invasion of, 101; Japanese occupation, 171 ff.; assassination of Chang Tso-lin, 174; "The Young Marshal," 176; conquest of, 176 ff.; railway treaties, 177; the League and, 178 ff., 191 f.; U. S. policy of non-recognition, 188 ff.
Mandates, 30; Japanese, 101
Manifest Destiny, 17
Massey, Vincent, 219
May, Sir George, 157
Mellon, Andrew W., 42, 67 f., 153; *re* reparations and war debts, 87; Seven-Power Conference, 156
Mercantilism, 14 f.
Mexican War, 11, 18
Mexico, 67; and Nicaragua, 211; revolt of 1929, 217; and the U. S., 201; dispute over American holdings in, 205 ff.
Midway, 101
Mills, Ogden, 137, 153, 167
Minami, Jiro, 176, 195
Mitsui and Mitsubishi, 175
Moncada, José Maria, 213
Monroe Doctrine, 8 ff.; Roosevelt corollary, 9, 211; Clark's memorandum on, 214
Moore, John Bassett, 112
Moratorium, *see* War debts
Morrison, C. C., 121
Morrow, Dwight W., 205; success in Mexico, 208 ff.
Most-favored-nation clause, 15 f.
Moulton, Harold G., 90
Mukden incident, 177 f.
Mussolini, Benito, 232

Nationalism, increase of, 98 f.
National Socialist Party (Nazis), 148; triumph in 1933 election, 164; U. S.-British plan to defeat, 234 f.
Naval Convention (1909), 14

Naval limitation, 97 ff., 127, 223 f.; in the Far East, 99; Far Eastern Conference (1921), 103 ff.; Conference of 1927, 120; London Conference (1930), 129 ff., 227; effect, in the Manchurian crisis, 183 ff.

Neutrality legislation, 1935–37, 13

Nicaragua, 18, 22; American intervention, 201 f., 210 ff.

Nicolson, Harold, quoted *re* Morrow in Mexico, 208

Nine-Power Treaty (1922), 14, 108, 178 f., 181, 191

Non-recognition, invoked by the U. S. *re* Manchuria, 188 ff.; the League and, 192

Obregon, Alvaro, 67, 206

Oil industry, in Mexico, 205 ff.

Open Door policy, 14, 24, 102, 188; Far Eastern Conference (1921), 104

Oregon, 18

Ottawa Imperial Conference, 143

Pact of Paris, *see* Kellogg-Briand Pact

Panama Canal, 201

Pan-American Conferences, 11, 219

Pan-Americanism, 10 ff.; Latin-American attitude toward, 201

Pan-American Union, 204 f.

Papen, Franz von, 164

Paraguay, Gran Chaco dispute, 218

Payne-Aldrich Tariff Act (1909), 142

Peace, international, policies toward, 95 ff.

Permanent Court of International Justice, 30; U. S. and, 51 f., 112 ff.

Peru, Tacna-Arica dispute, 217 f.

Philippines, 20, 101; independence of, 199 ff.

Phillips, William, 62, 219

Poincaré, Raymond, 89 f.

Political parties, U. S., and the League, 37 ff.

Presidential campaign (1920), 34

Privateering, 13

Pulitzer, Joseph, 19

Quezon, Manuel, 198

Quotas, international, 145

Rathenau, Walther, 233

Reading, Lord, 180

Reciprocal Tariff Act (1934), 16

Reparations, linked with war debts, 86 ff., 154 ff.; Lausanne settlement, 164

Republican party, and the League, 38 f., 47; and the World Court, 112; world disarmament conference, 100 ff.

Rhineland, occupation, 132

Robins, Raymond, 121

Rogers Act (1924), 64

Rogers, Grafton, 136

Rogers, John Jacob, 64

Rogers, Will, 209

Roosevelt, Franklin D., 5, 38, 167; problems faced by, 169; *re* independence of the Philippines, 198; *re* Haiti's constitution, 202

Roosevelt, Nicholas, *re* the Philippines, 198 f.

Roosevelt, Theodore, 201; corollary of the Monroe Doctrine, 9 f., 211; *re* treaties without enforcement, 96

Root, Elihu, 105; *re* the League, 38 f.; Nine-Power Treaty, 109; *re* foreign criticisms of the U. S., 235 f.

Root-Takahira Agreement, 80

Rubber, competitive market for, 76

Ruhr, occupation, 84 f., 89 f.

Russia, international losses on loans to, 69 f.; Japanese recognition of, 110; Comintern agents in China, 196 f.; reaction to army-ratio plan, 231

Sacasa, Juan B., 211, 213
St. Lawrence River waterway, 220
Salter, Sir Arthur, 209
Sanctions, economic, *see* Economic sanctions
Sandino, Augusto César, 213
Santo Domingo, 18, 22, 202
Schober, Johann, 147 f.
Seas, freedom of, 12 f.
Seven-Power Conference, 155 ff.
Shanghai, Japanese attack on, 190; reaction of world opinion, 192
Sheffield, James R., 207
Shidehara, Kijuru, 109, 171, 174, 178, 195
Shotwell, James T., 121, 125 f.
Simon, Sir John, 185 f., 189, 233
Sinclair, Harry F., 207
Smith, Alfred E., *re* the League, 117
Smoot-Hawley Tariff Act (1930), 140 ff.; effect on Japan, 174
Soong, Mei-ling, 173
Soong, T. V., 173
South America, U. S. investments, 75
South Manchurian Railway, 177 f.
Spain, Cortes, 180
Spanish War (1898), 24
Stanford University, Hoover Library, 4
Statute of Westminster, 180
Stevenson Plan, 75
Stimson, Henry L., 169; career, 135 f.; Seven-Power Conference, 156; note to France *re* war debts and reparations, 162 f.; and the Manchurian crisis, 178 ff.; Lloyd George *re*, 186; telephone conversations with Simon, 191; letter to Borah condemning Japan, 191 f.; mission to Nicaragua,

212 f.; European tour (1932), 232 f.
Stock market crash (1929), 137
Stresemann, Gustav, 118, 125
Sun Yat-sen, 172
Swanson, Claude A., 227
Sze, Alfred, 105

Tacna-Arica dispute, 133, 217 f.
Taft, William Howard, administration, 20 f.
Takahashi, Korekiyo, 171
Takahira, 80
Tanaka, Giichi, Baron, 171 f., "Memorial," 172; resignation, 174
Tariffs, discriminative, in world trade, 15; high, 66; Fordney-McCumber Act (1922), 72; Smoot-Hawley Act (1930), 140 ff., 174
Telephone, transatlantic, early use in foreign relations, 191
Territorial expansion, 17 ff.
Texas, 18; University of, 204
Thaelmann, Ernst, 163
Totalitarianism, 47 f.
Toynbee, Arnold, *re* the year 1931, 178

Ugaki, General, 176
Underwood, Oscar, 105
United States, foreign trade, 14 f., 93; relations with Canada, 23, 219 ff.; attitude toward the League, 30 ff., 57 ff., 99 f., 115 ff.; economic problems after World War I, 65 ff.; financial strength after World War I, 70 ff.; economic policy, 77 f.; and the war debts, 82 ff., 87 ff., 165 ff.; pre-depression world trade, 93; depression years, 137 ff.; economic quotas, 145 f.; bank failures, 158 f.; reaction to the Manchurian crisis, 178 ff.; effect of naval limitation on relations with Japan, 183 ff.; non-rec-

ognition of Japanese government in Manchuria, 188 ff.; Churchill *re* foreign policy of, 234; foreign criticisms of, 235 f.

——Foreign policy, traditions; history, 1 ff.; support of democracy, 5 ff., 46; and foreign alliances, 6 f.; freedom of the seas, 12 f.; liberalism vs. caution, 16 f.; territorial expansion, 17 f.; "dollar diplomacy," 20; toward Europe, 27 ff.; economic problems, 63 ff.; *see also under names of* Presidents and Secretaries of State

——and Latin America, 8 ff., 21 ff., 200 ff.; investments, 73, 202 ff.; armed intervention, 201 f., 210 ff., 215 ff.; cultural relations, 204; settlement of disputes, 217 f.; *see also* Monroe Doctrine

U. S. Navy, air force, 184; *see also* Naval limitation

U. S. Senate, and the League, 31 ff.; Foreign Relations Committee, 34; attitude toward the World Court, 112 ff.; and the Hoover moratorium, 162

Uriburu, José, 146

Vargas, Getulio, 146
Versailles, Treaty of, 223, 228
Vincent, Stenio, 216
Viviani, René, 105

Wages, 71
Wakatsuki, Reijiiro, Baron, 195
War, outlawry of, 95 ff., 121 ff., 187; American draft treaty, 122 f.
War debts, 68 ff.; U. S. vs. Allied policy, 82 ff.; Baldwin-Mellon agreement, 85 ff.; Hoover moratorium, 153 ff.; Lausanne "gentlemen's agreement" *re,* 165; *see also* Reparations

War Debts Commission, 86
War of 1812, 18
Washington, George, Farewell Address, 6 f.
Webster, Daniel, 5
Weeks, John W., 43
Western powers, opportunities to halt Japan, 179 ff., 194 f.
Wheeler, Burton K., 161
White, Henry, 32
White, William Allen, 216
Wickersham, George, 235; quoted, 45
Wiggin, Albert H., 156
Wilson, Hugh, 178
Wilson, Woodrow, *re* American isolationism, 5; Fourteen Points, 12, 16; *re* Latin America, 22; and the League, 31 f., 50; illness, 33 f.; prediction of World War II, 59; administration, 67; *re* emergency tariff, 72; interventionist policy, 216 f.

Woolley, Mary, 227
World Court, *see* Permanent Court of International Justice
World Economic Conference (1927), 120 f.
World market, *see* International trade
World War I, change in U. S. foreign policy, 4; U. S. effort, 34 f.; losses, 36; economic problems following, 65 f.
Young, Owen D., 88, 153
Young Plan, 90 ff., 132

Zinoviev, Grigori E., 133